Not Quite Burned Out But Crispy Around the Edges

D0188210

Other books by Sharon Draper

Teaching from the Heart
0-325-00131-6

Tears of a Tiger
0-689-31878-2 (hb)
0-689-80698-1 (pb)

Forged by Fire
0-689-80699-X (hb)
0-689-81851-3 (pb)

Darkness Before Dawn
0-689-83080-7 (hb)

Romiette and Julio
0-689-82180-8 (hb)
0-689-84209-0 (pb)

Jazzimagination
0-439-06130-X

Ziggy and the Black Dinosaurs
0-940-97548-3

Lost in the Tunnel of Time
0-940-97563-7

Shadows of Caesar's Creek
0-940-97576-9

Not Quite Burned Out
But Crispy Around the Edges

Inspiration, Laughter, and
Encouragement for Teachers

Sharon M. Draper

HEINEMANN
Portsmouth, NH

Heinemann
A division of Reed Elsevier Inc.
361 Hanover Street
Portsmouth, NH 03801-3912
www.heinemann.com

Offices and agents throughout the world

© 2001 by Sharon M. Draper

All rights reserved. No part of this book may be reproduced in any form or by any electronic or mechanical means, including information storage and retrieval systems, without permission in writing from the publisher, except by a reviewer, who may quote brief passages in a review.

The author and publisher wish to thank those who have generously given permission to reprint borrowed material:

"One Small Torch" first appeared as a short story in *Ebony* magazine in January 1991 and was the first-prize winner in the 1990 Gertrude Williams Johnson Literary Contest.

"One Small Torch" also appears as Chapter 1 in *Forged by Fire* by Sharon M. Draper. Copyright © 1997 by Sharon M. Draper. Published in hardcover by Atheneum Books for Young Readers and in paperback by Aladdin Paperbacks.

Library of Congress Cataloging-in-Publication Data

Draper, Sharon M. (Sharon Mills)
    Not quite burned out but crispy around the edges : inspiration, laughter, and encouragement for teachers / Sharon Draper.
      p. cm.
    ISBN 0-325-00365-3 (pbk.)
     1. Teaching. 2. High school teachers—United States—
    Anecdotes. I. Title.
LB1025.3 .D73 2001
371.102—dc21
                                     2001020423

Editor: Lois Bridges
Production: Elizabeth Valway
Cover design: Jenny Jensen Greenleaf
Manufacturing: Steve Bernier

Printed in the United States of America on acid-free paper
05 04 03 02 01 DA 1 2 3 4 5

This book is dedicated to all teachers—
the candles in the darkness,
the wisdom in the wind—
those who know that teaching is sometimes
like watching frozen honey melt
and drip into your waiting palm—
so agonizingly slow,
yet so sweet when it finally happens.

Contents

Preface
Remembering the Joy

D o you ever have trouble remembering the reason why you went into teaching in the first place? Was it the joy? The passion? The excitement about the possibility of stimulating young minds? Have you ever been awakened by your alarm clock, only to lie in the semidarkness wondering why you should even bother to get up and go to school one more day? *Not Quite Burned Out, But Crispy Around The Edges* was written for you. None of us anticipate burnout, but sometimes, over the years, it creeps up on us slowly as necessity and reality gradually overpower our youthful enthusiasm and optimism.

This book of inspirational stories and essays is designed for any teacher who has survived the first week of the first year of teaching. It offers memories of the joy of teaching, tells memorable tales of tragedy as well as survival, and provides opportunities for laughter, which is sometimes the only remedy for difficult situations.

Teachers face low salaries, large classes, crumbling buildings, and dwindling public support. We are asked to improve student performance, answer public scrutiny, and solve all of society's problems with just a stroke of chalk across a blackboard. It is easy to get discouraged and quit, and many do. This book is designed to scrape away the crunchy edges, and remind us all of the beauty and glory of what we as teachers do every day.

I have been very blessed in my educational career. I taught English language, literature, and composition for thirty years in junior and senior high schools, where I did my best to make magic of the words my students read and those they created on paper. I was the National Teacher of the Year in 1997, and was fortunate enough to travel all over the country, doing my best to encourage and inspire teachers with praise and recognition. In addition, I have written several books for young people that are now required reading in schools all over the country. As an English teacher who for years had a required list of books for my students to read, it is humbling and awesome to know that my books are now included on many of those lists.

I know what it's like to be there in the classroom. I know the frustration as well as the satisfaction of working with young people. Sometimes all we need is a reminder of why we do what we do each day. Sometimes we need an inspirational boost to remember the love and passion that ultimately motivate us all.

One of the best ways to remind each other of the value of what we do is through the telling of stories. Since ancient times, human beings have shared tales of adventure and sorrow and laughter to bind them together. I've tried to include tales of tears, inspiration, humor, and wisdom. All of the stories about schools and teachers that I recount in these pages are true, except for, of course, the story of the dragon and the story of the tapestries. I have traveled across the country, and I've had the opportunity to visit hundreds of schools and observe in dozens of classrooms and lunchrooms and teachers' rooms. In all cases I have changed the names of the teachers and students involved to protect their identity and privacy.

We all need validation and reassurance. I wrote this book just for you. Hang in there! We need you. The students need you. And, believe it or not, you need them as well. Peace.

Sharon M. Draper

1

The Ninety-Seventh Day of Your Seventeenth Year of Teaching

A Day Like All the Others—And That's the Problem

It's Monday, it's February, and you have a cold. You pull the collar of your brown coat closer to you as you hurry across the parking lot. You hate that brown coat, the one you bought on sale last September when the weather was still warm and winter seemed liked a pleasant vacation to look forward to. You hate it because it reminds you of cold and dreariness and mud—mud all over your classroom floor by the end of the morning.

You hurry into the fluorescent warmth of the teachers' workroom and find that the copier is broken, again. A hastily scribbled note tells you the repairman has been called. It was working when you left on Friday, but it was the end of the week and you were tired, and you promised yourself you'd come in early on Monday and beat the crowd and run off your lessons for the day. You look at the faces of your colleagues, who are staring at you and not smiling. You wonder why. You cannot deal with them without coffee so you turn to make yourself a cup—black and steamy. You never drank coffee before you started teaching—but now your day cannot begin without it. You glance with dismay at the cold and empty coffee machine. Whose turn was it anyway to fill it this week? You angrily check the coffee list tacked on the wall to find out which thoughtless person on the staff is about to get a piece of your mind. You discover it was you. You tiptoe to the other side of the workroom and silently admire your colleagues, who had said nothing about your oversight. They've been teaching longer than you have.

You decide to use the one computer they have installed in the teachers' workroom and print out some materials you can use in your classroom today. When you click the ON button, all you hear is a strange clunking noise. A colleague shouts from across the room, "Computer's down, too." They tell you a repairman has been called for that machine as well. You figure both of them are in a pleasant little café, casually reading the morning paper and sipping the coffee you forgot to bring.

You decide to type your lesson materials on the Olivetti Underwood typewriter covered with dust in the far corner of the workroom. You knew there was a reason they left that thing in there. What button do you push to make it return? What do you mean I have to do it *manually*? Bummer. I spelled something wrong. How do you delete? What do mean you can't delete? My whole life is a deletion!

You wonder what time it is. In your haste to get to work early, you left your watch at home. You glance at the clock on the wall of the workroom. It's first thing in the morning and the clock says 2:00. A.M. or P.M.? Not sure. You go out into the hall. The clock there says 9:00. You stick your head into the closest classroom. The clock there says it's either noon or midnight. No two clocks in the building have the same time. The bells ring anyway.

It's time for first bell and you turn on the lights in your classroom. You inhale deeply and just for a moment you are filled with the giddy exhilaration of the first day of school when everything was new and fresh and ready to blossom. You glance around the room and notice Lisa's book bag on the floor where she left it Friday, the torn window shades, which have never, in your ten years at that school, been repaired, and the bulletin board on which are tacked faces of great American heroes. You sigh and get ready for the day.

You look for your grade book in the canvas bag that says, "I Teach America's Future." You're having trouble dealing with America's present at the moment. You remember that report cards are due at the end of the week and you still have sixteen stacks of paper to record in your grade book. Where is that book anyway? You remember then that the grade book is at home. Under the bed. Where it slid off after you fell asleep grading those papers at midnight. You sigh once more and the bell for first period rings.

The kids troop in, doing everything that you have told them not to do since the first day of school. You tell Paulo to remove his hat, Larry to remove his sunglasses, and Rita to spit out her gum. Every day. Since you don't have your grade book, you can't officially record the attendance, but they don't know it, so you fake it. You'll record it tomorrow, along with the ever-growing stack of papers.

You finally get them settled down and involved in a lesson that was not exactly what you had intended to do today, but you've been teaching long enough to have alternative plans for just about any situation. The kids are quiet, interested, busily engaged, when the public address system interrupts. "Attention, please. It is now time to bring all classes to the auditorium for the assembly." In the three seconds it took to say, "Attention, please," the students had eliminated your lesson from their mind, packed their book bags, and huddled at the door to leave. You remember vaguely that this assembly had been announced three weeks ago. You toss your lesson plans into the canvas bag where you keep your life, and you join the hordes of students in the hall, trying in vain to find your class and keep them together.

At the assembly you lean against the wall because it is solid and does not move. The other teachers are lined up with you at five-foot intervals, leaning, occasionally giving instructions to students in the seats. But the wall is your resting place for a few minutes, until the assembly is over and classes are dismissed to their next bell. The assembly was a band concert—lots of loud, military-style music—cymbals crashing and drums booming. Just the thing to stimulate kids first thing in the morning. You must remember to thank the administration.

You begin second bell, which is the same as first bell and third bell and fifth bell—eighth graders—and you make a mental note that somehow you must catch the first-bell class up to the material you are covering with the rest of the eighth-grade classes, but deep down you know it will never come out even. The kids are noisy and excited because of the assembly. You finally settle them down and manage to get through half of what you had planned for the day. You discover that Elaine, your best student—the one who smiled at you every morning and never forgot her homework, the one whose papers you graded first because they were always so thoughtful and refreshing—has moved to Oregon with her family. You envy the teachers of Oregon.

The third-bell class is in an uproar because the students have heard that their lunch period next year will be ten minutes shorter. Full of righteous indignation, they want to capitalize on their rights as citizens—from that chapter of their history book they slept through, claiming it boring—and write petitions and picket and have a protest rally. You admire their youthful energy, calm them down, and explain that the changes proposed for next year will not really affect their lunch time because other parts of the schedule have added flexibility. As usual, they have jumped to conclusions because of incomplete information, but you applaud them for trying to incorporate some of the ideas you have been trying to teach, even though you know the only reason they wanted to have a protest rally was to get out of classes. No student ever scheduled a protest rally after school.

Fourth bell is your lunch period, where you get to eat your lunch standing up while monitoring the behavior of four hundred children in a hot, overcrowded cafeteria. You almost choke on your tuna fish sandwich as you see Jackie and Brick and Connie tossing Jell-O cubes across the floor. You move to intercept the most recent toss and it hits you on the neck. You survive the assault. Instead of sending Jackie to the office, which would do no good at this time of day, you make her clean up the Jell-O, which by now is squished under the feet of dozens of kids. You glance at the clock and have no idea how much longer you must endure this because that clock, too, is out of order. You sip on a juice box and hope there's toilet paper in the teachers' bathroom.

Fifth bell, you repeat yourself once more, trying hard to remember what you said in the last two classes, trying to make sure you have included all the material the other students received, even the jokes you told. You give up trying to remember, and just teach, telling yourself that you'll make up five different tests for the five different classes, which basically covers the same material. But you know you won't. And if you do, the copier will be down again.

When the bell rings and the class leaves, you quietly ask Ben to stay a moment. You tell him you are concerned about his grades, which are dismal, and his attitude, which is even worse. You offer support and encouragement, and reach out to touch his shoulder, but you decide not to. He is bristling with adolescent anger and confusion. As he stalks away, he mumbles, "Stupid teacher makes me sick," just loud enough for you to hear. Instead of being dismayed, you are wise enough to know you have struck a chord, touched him just a little. You promise yourself to find something for him to do that will build his self-esteem without making him lose any dignity in front of his peers.

Sixth bell, you have a planning period where the idea is that you consult with other teachers and plan for your day. What? Today is shot and tomorrow is a full twenty-four hours away. Besides, your feet hurt, you have a throbbing headache, and you must get to the phone so you can call the phone company to let them know you dropped the check in the mail this morning. It's not that you didn't have the money—you just forgot to write the check, then you forgot where you put the stamps, then you tossed it into that big canvas bag and it was lost for a week or so, and when you found it, it was covered with old cookie crumbs and you took it to the mailbox. The lady at the phone company would never have believed the truth.

You also call three parents—all you really have time for. Danny's mother answers on the first ring. You can hear the voices of families in crisis on a daytime talk show screaming in the background. You speak loudly and repeat yourself several times because Danny's mother is paying more attention to the television than she is to you. But she gets the message that Danny is struggling and probably needs glasses. You hang up and sigh, exhausted from the conversation. Your headache is worse. You call LeeAnn's home and leave a message. LeeAnn has stopped doing homework. You call Tristan's home, but the phone has been disconnected. You make a mental note to write a letter, but you know you'll probably forget to do so.

As the bell rings for seventh bell, you notice the copy-repair person—a woman—has arrived. She looks rested and relaxed. You look like you feel—tired, drained, and frazzled. You consider asking her about openings in the copy-repair business.

Seventh bell, your last class, is the only class that is a different grade and preparation from your other classes. These kids probably would be great if you saw them first thing in the morning. But by the end of the day, they are dragging, tired, and lethargic. The sugar they had at lunch has long since disappeared from their bloodstreams and you usually need a cannon to get their attention. You appreciate the break in the monotony of the instruction, but you, too, would be better with them if you saw them first thing in the morning. You search in your canvas bag for a piece of peppermint. You find one piece, only a little dirty, and you pop it in your mouth for energy and headache relief. It works, because it must.

You get the class settled, wake them up, even get them interested in a lesson that surprises even you in how well they are responding. They are raising their hands with excitement and enthusiasm, asking questions that actually make sense, and learning—you can see the little cogs turning in their brains. You can see the material going in and watch it come out as learned, digested knowledge. It's amazing, marvelous, one of those days you'll always treasure because at one perfect moment in time you found the magic flow of teaching and learning.

Suddenly, "WHEEEEEEEEEE"—the fire bell sounds and the magic is instantly destroyed—gone like a bubble that has exploded in a breeze. You troop out of the building, down the steps, across the street, "quietly and quickly now," to the designated waiting area until the all-clear bell is sounded. You wonder angrily why they wait until the end of the day to have a fire drill, when you notice the fire trucks near the front entrance. You remember that once a month the fire chief is required to pull the bell at all the schools. Today was just your lucky day. You march back in with your students when the all-clear bell sounds, but the magic is gone. You give up any hope of recapturing their attention or minds.

You assign the homework, give them the last five minutes to "study," and sit down at your desk for the first time all day.

The bell finally rings at the end of the day, and hundreds of lethargic, disinterested children somehow immediately find energy and life once more as they rush into the halls to go home. You slowly gather your belongings together, and stuff one more set of papers, which you vow you will grade tonight—no excuses—into your bag. You head to the workroom to find that the computer and the copier are still broken down. A note attached to one, from the repair person, cheerfully states she will be back next week with the needed parts. You put on your hated brown coat and head toward the door, when the public address system loudly bleats, "Attention, please! Teachers are reminded of the faculty meeting today. Please report promptly to the meeting room."

You had forgotten, of course, about the meeting. You seriously consider leaving, skipping out early, but you sigh, grab your overloaded bag, and head to the meeting. You pick up an agenda at the front door, read it quickly, and realize that every item on it could have been covered in a typed memo that might have taken five minutes to read and absorb. But you sit and listen to instructions about how to administer the standardized tests, how to fill in the bubble sheets for the new computer system, and how the parking lot will be resurfaced tomorrow and you will have to find a parking place on the surrounding streets. Nothing instructional or useful is covered in this meeting, and you sigh, and wish you had a watch, for the clock on the wall in the meeting room has no hands at all. Just as the meeting is almost over and the principal is shuffling papers to put back into his briefcase, he asks casually, "Are there any questions?" The room is silent—everyone daring anyone to speak.

From the back of the room, a hand is raised. Looks try to kill the hand's owner. "Could you please explain the procedure for parent contact in case of a schoolwide emergency? It was number four on the agenda and you skipped it."

The principal smiles and says, "Thank you for reminding me," and proceeds to go into great detail about the telephone tree. The answer takes seventeen minutes.

You are finally dismissed and you head to the parking lot, dragged down, worn out, and not even sure why you showed up today. You don't think you are burned out like some of your friends who have lost all joy and pleasure in teaching, but you're afraid you're approaching that point. You're feeling not quite burned out, but like you're getting a little crispy around your edges. You feel like a pie that has been left in the oven a little too long. Your crust, which was once baked to perfection, is starting to show signs of being overcooked. Too much heat and too much pressure for way too long. You fear what will happen if you don't get out of this kitchen pretty soon.

A young woman approaches you as you reach your car. "Hi! Remember me?" she says cheerfully. You do, but only vaguely. You remember the face, when it was longer, more innocent, thinner. Strangely, you somehow remember her handwriting—how she dotted all her I's with little hearts. But you can't remember her name.

Nevertheless, you smile broadly and say, "Yes! How are you? What are you doing now?" She seems to understand that you need a memory push, so she tells you her name and how many years ago you had her in class. It all comes back—that class, that year, that student. You remember doodles and drawings on the sides of all her papers. You remember she had sad eyes. She tells you she is an artist, working for a large greeting card company, happily doing work she loves. Her eyes are no longer sad.

She says, "I just wanted to let you know that you changed my life. I was an unhappy child, and coming to your class was always fun. Of all my teachers, you were the only one who made me laugh, took the time to talk to me, gave me encouragement. Because of you, I didn't give up. Because of you, I made it through. I'm so glad you're still here and still teaching. I wonder if your students today know how lucky they are to have you as their teacher."

You are stunned, almost speechless. Here is a young woman you had forgotten, a faint blip on your memory screen. But in her mind, *you* were the dominant memory. You were the reason she made it as a human being. She hugs you, thanks you, gets back into her car, and drives away.

You stand there in the almost empty parking lot, a little overwhelmed. You glance at the building, take a deep breath, and smile. You hurry home because you have much to do. Tomorrow is another day and you get to do it all over again. You can't wait.

2

Once upon a Time Was a Long Time Ago

Kids and Reading

Remember Campus tablets and Laddie pencils? The smell of new Crayola crayons, which came with a sharpener if you were lucky enough to get the big box of sixty-four, which carried a delicious assortment of colors and possibilities? Remember when desks were nailed to the floor and the Pledge of Allegiance was recited every morning after the singing of "God Bless America"? Remember the window pole, which was used to pull down the huge windows? The pencil sharpener? The cloak room?

Remember when only boys took woodworking and shop, and only girls took sewing and cooking? Remember Dick and Jane or Alice and Jerry, the children of the early readers who were our role models for families, whether we wanted them to be or not?

Remember when every story began with "once upon a time" and ended with "happily ever after"? Fair damsels were rescued by blond, bland heroes on white horses. Dragons were slain, villains were vanquished, and good always conquered evil.

So much has changed. "Once upon a time" was a long time ago. Children of twenty or fifty years ago were fascinated and mesmerized by those words, which conjured up thoughts of castles and mysteries, heroes and villains, princes and monsters and dreams. Children today, however, may have never even heard those words, and are much more in tune to the theme song of a television program. Many kids today don't read much, and they don't read well. They learn to read in school, basically, but many times they don't learn to *love* reading in the process.

A child just learning to read and successfully mastering the process finds great joy in the victory of the battle to decipher those marks on a page of text. Many very young children have a large variety of sight words in their vocabulary from the prominent advertising of fast-food restaurants, bottled sodas, and brand-name athletic clothing. They know the products and ask for them by name. The power in the knowledge, and the rewards that come with the connection between the symbol and the product are established and reinforced very early. As reading educators, and all of us, regardless of what we teach, are reading teachers, we must build on this positive synergy that already exists by expanding it into the classroom and beyond.

I met a remarkable young teacher named Sandy who worked with disadvantaged third graders in Chicago. Most of them scored very low on standardized reading and vocabulary tests but were surprisingly verbal and articulate. She quizzed them on brand names and, not surprisingly, they scored one hundred percent. She decided that the only solution was to teach them by using their rules instead of hers, their knowledge base instead of her own. So she and her students invented and created a town.

The town had a restaurant with golden arches, but the name of the place was "Delectable Delights," and it served "Magnificent Morsels." The town had sweet, brown cola drinks with red labels, but the drinks were called "Literary Thirst Quenchers." The tiny used-car lot they built was called "Automobiles for Consumers." The entire town, which the children painted and built themselves, was filled with familiar brand designs that were labeled with increasingly difficult vocabulary words. The streets were lined with verbs and the road signs were adjectives and adverbs. The children, who before had no interest at all in reading or learning, daily brought new words and new ways to include them in their town design, constantly expanding their town. They learned city planning, community and social interaction, and the value of reading as well. By the end of the year, the children knew thousands of new words, how to put them together into meaningful sentences, and how to recognize those words, even when they were not attached to a familiar label. Their reading scores soared, as did their self-esteem and success in other classes.

Sometimes, however, a child needs individual attention, and no amount of classroom creativity will work. I remember a student the kids called Brownie. Her last name was Brown, but everything about her was brown and muddy-looking, from her clothes to her eyes to her scuffed shoes. Her face was a ruddy-brown, chocolate color, not deep and luscious like a Hershey's chocolate kiss, but mottled and dry, like a piece of chocolate that had been left outside its wrapper too long. Her hair was a dusty brown color, usually unbrushed and unkempt. Brownie's personality was mottled and muddy as well. She was very quiet, and when she talked, she held her head low and mumbled. I had to resist the urge to take her home with me, brush and shine her hair, feed her, and care for her. I loved to see her smile, which was rare.

Brownie hated to read. She stumbled over words when we acted out plays in class, and her silent reading was painstakingly slow as she put her fingers under every single word. By seventh grade, there is no longer the support of reading groups, which usually means the beginning of the end for kids like Brownie, who never mastered reading.

I told her I needed a student assistant and asked if she'd be interested in the job. She looked surprised that I would select her, but shyly agreed to help me out. Every day during fourth bell she came into my room, where she sorted papers or washed the boards or stacked books, much of which I could have done quite well without her. But we talked and, after I broke through her initial shyness, I found a wonderful twelve-year-old girl who had imagination and dreams like all the other kids her age, but who was afraid to show any of that because of her fear of reading. I let her read to me—out loud, with no other students around to giggle and point, and slowly she gained courage as well as skill. At first I only asked her to read sections from the newspaper, the TV Guide, and the comics. Later, she read her homework to me from other classes. Gradually, she read me little stories she had written and illustrated herself. We got to be friends that year, and Brownie's social as well as academic skills improved greatly. She moved away at the end of the school year, but before she left, she gave me a hug as well as that smile I loved. I'm willing to bet that no one called her "Brownie" at her new school.

Kids today live in a noisy, frenetic world of instant gratification and electronic satisfaction. Information they need can be instantly downloaded from their computers to their printers without having to pass through their brains for thought or digestion of ideas. Their worlds are hurried, pushed, and scheduled. They go to soccer practice, ballet lessons, and gymnastics. They heat their dinners in the microwave, watch television while paying cursory attention to homework, then fall asleep in exhaustion and start the routine again the next day.

I had this conversation last week with a seventh grader named Jack at a school in California:

SD: So, how do you like school? (I realize this is a stupid question to ask a seventh grader. What did I expect him to say, "I love it! It's my ultimate fantasy!"?)

Jack: It's OK. Sorta boring.

SD: What's your favorite subject?

Jack: Lunch.

SD: What's your favorite academic subject?

Jack: Gym.

SD: Do you like to read?

Jack: No.

SD: I guess I should have asked what's your favorite thing to read.

Jack: Nothing at school.

SD: OK, what do you like to read outside of school?

Jack: Baseball cards.

SD: Do you play baseball?

Jack: Yeah, I play first base.

SD: I bet you're really good at it.

Jack: (finally smiling) Yeah, I'm really good. Nobody gets past me.

SD: Do you go to practice often?

Jack: Every day after school. Games on weekends.

SD: Do you play any other sport?

Jack: Football and basketball.

SD: All three? You must be a really good athlete. After practice, is that when you do your homework?

Jack: Sometimes. But sometimes I get busy playing video games and I forget.

SD: You have a video game player in your room?

Jack: Yeah.

SD: A TV and VCR?

Jack: Yeah.

SD: A CD player?

Jack: Yeah.

SD: Computer and printer?

Jack: Yeah. I have a cell phone and a pager too.

SD: Do most of your friends have all those things as well?

Jack: Yeah, most of them.

SD: So I'm still trying to find out about reading. When do you read?

Jack: I don't.

SD: Why not?

Jack: I told you—it's boring.

Their world has very little time for leisurely, extended periods of reading. Nothing in our current way of living encourages, applauds, or celebrates the joy of reading. The joy of television, the glory of movies, the magic of video images—these are what our society celebrates and emulates. So of course, children today grow up with minimal reading skills and minimal reading joy. By the time they get to junior high, the enjoyment of reading is completely atrophied; when given the choice, many young people with an extra fifteen dollars to spend will buy a compact music disc instead of a book. That young person will watch a television show instead of read a book. It is a difficult, but not insurmountable problem.

One ninth-grade English teacher named Edith came up with a cleverly designed solution. Edith had been teaching for almost thirty years. She had seen the gradual slide in literacy over the years and she struggled valiantly, but usually unsuccessfully, to thwart the increasing presence of television in the lives of her students. Finally she had an inspiration. Instead of fighting television, she decided to use it.

First, she gave homework assignments that required her students to watch television intelligently. Her students were amazed initially, telling their parents exultantly, "The teacher told us we GOTTA watch TV tonight!" She had them watching news shows, counting commercials, and keeping records of weather reports.

But Edith didn't stop there. Each student got to choose a television program and analyze it, from the script writing, to the actors, to the show's effectiveness. The students then had to write to the producers and directors and others whose names appeared in the credits of their shows to find out all kinds of detailed information about the structure and the function of the program. As letters began to pour in, the students were amazed at the sincerity of the responses and the complexity of the industry they were now investigating and discovering. All the while, students were using reading and writing skills effectively, and they were totally unaware that they were doing so because they were having so much fun in the process.

Finally, Edith had her students write, produce, and direct their own television show, which included commercials, a theme song, actors, directors, and sponsors. Parents with video cameras and recorders supplied the equipment. That year Edith's students learned that reading and writing are essential to prepare for the very active world that they had formerly watched so passively. Edith survived one more year of ninth grade, and her students' lives were changed forever.

In order to make reading palatable as well as profitable for students today, educators must make reading as fashionable as the latest designer shoes, as desirable as the most popular fast food, and as valuable as the most high-tech video game. It's all in the marketing. Kids desire items because slick advertising campaigns, designed to manipulate their minds, are extremely successful. Reading, which is the key to a world of knowledge beyond that commercialism, must compete with and conquer the forces that push it to the bottom of the book bag in the priority system of students today.

I once had a class of tenth graders, most of whom where nonreaders. All of them had repeated at least a year of school and all of them were over sixteen. They had no interest at all in *A Tale of Two Cities,* but all of them wanted to drive. So we read the manual put out by the state of Ohio to prepare drivers for their test. We learned vocabulary, grammar, and comprehension skills from the booklet. That year, they all passed their driver's test, they all mastered driving, and they all increased their reading skills in spite of themselves. Later, we even managed to tackle *A Tale of Two Cities,* with a bit more interest and success this time around. (We started with research on the guillotine and how it works. After that, I had their attention!)

If we start with children while they are very young and encourage in them the love of reading, if we nurture that love throughout their school careers, perhaps we can make a difference, a rip in the blanket of disinterest they hide under. Here's a little rhythm piece I started using with younger children, but perhaps not surprisingly, adolescents love it as well. It's called "Reader's Rap."

Say hey hey!   (teacher yells with enthusiasm)
I read a book today!

 Say hey hey!   (children yell back in response)
 I read a book today!

Say yo yo!   (teacher yells with enthusiasm)
I'm gonna read some mo'!

 Say yo yo!   (children yell back in response)
 I'm gonna read some mo'!

In a book I find the magic
In a book I find the key

When I read my brain is busy
When I read my mind is free

Say hey hey!
I read a book today!
　Say hey hey!
　I read a book today!

Say yo yo!
I'm gonna read some mo'!
　Say yo yo!
　I'm gonna read some mo'!

In a book I find the answers
In a book I find the clues
When I read I am the captain
When I read I NEVER LOSE!

Say hey hey!
I read a book today!
　Say hey hey!
　I read a book today!

Say yo yo!
I'm gonna read some mo'!
　Say yo yo!
　I'm gonna read some mo'!

With a book I have the victory
With a book I have a friend
With a book I am a champion
With a book I always win!

Say hey hey!
I read a book today!
　Say hey hey!
　I read a book today!

Say yo yo!
I'm gonna read some mo'!
Say yo yo!
I'm gonna read some mo'!

The vision of hundreds, or thousands, of classrooms around the country filled with children who love learning and who are passionate about reading is not a misty, impossible dream. It is an achievable reality. If we can market shoes or hamburgers or T-shirts to our children, then certainly we can market reading as effectively. If television producers can create scenarios that capture the minds of our children, we can utilize that medium to our benefit. If we take the time to create the magic of reading and let it work in our classrooms, we can create readers and lovers of reading. Teachers like Sandy and Edith and hundreds like them are erasing the negatives and building on the positives to help kids learn to read—not just for necessity, but for pleasure. Kids like Brownie, or Jack, or my tenth graders, can feel victorious and proud. "Once upon a time" can belong to our children once more.

3

The Broom Brigade

The Power of Parents and Teachers

One of the least favorite, but most necessary, jobs of the teacher is calling parents. We are given perhaps a forty-minute free bell, during which we must try to contact the parents of children who are disruptive, or are frequently absent, or seem to have a particular need. We would love to call the parents of students who are doing remarkably well, or who have improved, but usually there is not enough time because those students who are having problems need all of our time and attention.

As a parent of four children, I never got the following phone call, although I wish I had:

"Hello, this is your son's teacher."

"What has he done now?"

"Nothing. He's doing great."

"Then why did you call? Does he owe money for something?"

"No, I just called to let you know that your son is an excellent student and a delight to have in class."

I probably would have fainted. First, because my sons were often "creative challenges" to their teachers and I honored those teachers for even attempting to teach them. When one of my sons was in third grade, he put a frog on the piano keys then closed the key cover. When his music teacher opened it to begin class, the frog jumped out, the teacher screamed, and the kids rolled with laughter. She was not amused. I got the phone call to prove it.

Second, I would have been surprised to get a positive phone call from one of my children's teachers because I know that teachers rarely have the time to make such wonderfully warming phone calls. I admit that as teacher I did not make as many of those as I should have. Not even close. I had so many wonderful students, but like many of us, I tended to take them for granted because the children with problems take precedence, and we use what little time we can squeeze into our day to call as many of their parents as possible.

You find a free chair, hope a phone line is available, make the first call, and realize that the phone number is either incorrect or has been changed. You call the next number on your list. An answering machine responds. You leave a message, knowing that when the return call comes, you will probably be in class and will miss it. You try to leave a message that says to call you at 2:00 P.M. because that is the only time you know for sure you will be available. You know you will play phone tag for several days and the child's problem needs to be addressed immediately. You make the next call and the grandmother answers. She doesn't speak English very well, but she is very concerned and promises to relay your message to the parents. The next number is a work number. A secretary answers and informs you that the father is away from his desk. You leave a message asking the father to call, stressing that is not an emergency because you don't want the parent to think the child has fallen off the swings again. You finally connect on the next call and the parent, who is very concerned, talks for thirty minutes. Your free period is over and you have called only five of the twenty-seven parents on your list.

Parents are often intimidated by the massive bureaucracy that schools exhibit. We send them forms to fill out and letters to sign. We send them notices about candy sales and book fees and assemblies and vacations. We send letters about school policies and we tell them their visit is always welcome, but it isn't. And sometimes we discourage them when they dare to venture into our territory.

Parent: I came here today to visit my son's classes.

Administrator: Do you have an appointment?

Parent: No, I just want to see his classes. Is that OK?

Administrator: It's fine, just a little unusual. Are you sure you don't want to come back another time? We're having a busy day.

Parent: Is there anything I can do to help?

Administrator: Have a seat. I'll check with the secretaries.

Parents are a valuable asset and we should encourage them to help us whenever they can. They can assist on field trips, work in the library or nurse's office, tutor, or even help in the classroom as an unofficial teachers' assistant. Students in elementary schools love to see their parents in the schools. Once they hit puberty, however, they would rather eat live snakes than see their parent walking down the halls of their school. Parents generally know this and are often more reluctant to continue to volunteer on school-related projects as their children get older. Older students, however, need their parents to be involved as much as their younger siblings. We sometimes have to be creative with how this is accomplished.

One high school I know of has a very strong parent-tutor program. It works because the young people are directed *away* from their parents and *toward* parents of other students in other grades. High school kids generally feel that they can open up to any adult except for parents; this school knows that and uses it to their advantage. They have ice cream socials and pizza parties; they have "switch nights" where the students take on the roles of the parents and the parents become kids. It is great fun, and increases everyone's appreciation for the school and its programs. And of course, everyone loves pizza and ice cream.

Some schools have difficulty getting any parents to participate, for a variety of reasons. I was involved in a project recently where the school actively sought out parents considered to be "uncaring" because they did not attend the various functions and events of the school. An informal survey sent to parents who did not participate in any of the school activities brought some interesting responses:

- We love our kids and don't like being singled out as uncaring.
- I know my kid better than anyone else. Ask me. I'll tell you what you need to know.
- I would go to school more if I could. I have no transportation. If you come to my house, I will treat you like a guest. But you never come.
- Who's going to take care of my other kids? I would come if you had some kind of baby-sitting service.
- I want my kids to do real good in school. They don't want me there.
- I want my kids to be happy and successful and have a better life, an easier life than I did. It is your job to make that happen.

- I like the school, but I don't feel like I'm really wanted there. Some of the other parents act like snobs.
- I have to work every day. School is out when I get off. There's not much I can do.
- I'm involved, but by telephone. Does that count?
- I hated school when I was a kid. Schools make me uncomfortable.
- I was never very successful in school. I'm afraid the teachers will think I'm stupid and my kids will be embarrassed.
- Nobody has ever called me to ask for my help.
- I figured I'd just be in the way. I don't know much about "school stuff."
- The school has too many problems. I am just one person. I can't solve them. When you get things straight, I'll show up.

I once met with a group of parents from an urban school district who were upset with the conditions of the schools in their neighborhood. Urban decay, poor city planning, and overwhelming despair had made the local school yard look something close to a junkyard. Broken bottles lined the asphalt, which had grass, weeds, even small trees sprouting from it. Litter, garbage, and an abandoned car cluttered the place where the children had to play. They had come to complain.

One mother loudly proclaimed with disgust, "It's criminal how filthy they keep that school yard! They ought to do something about that!" The other parents, full of indignation, agreed.

Instead of addressing her complaints, which were valid and right, I asked her, "Do you own a broom?"

Surprised into silence, she looked at me like I was crazy and said, "Yes, of course."

"Do all of you have brooms?" I asked the rest of them. Sensing what I was going to say, they warily indicated that they did, indeed, own brooms.

"And shovels and rakes and garbage cans?"

They nodded.

"Then let's form a Broom Brigade!" I announced with enthusiasm. "Are you going to wait until someone else gets around to solving your problem when you have the ability to solve it yourselves? Are you going to wait until one of your children are injured before you do something? You want the school yard cleaned? So clean it up!"

They looked at me in wonder at first, then they warmed to the idea. I could see the enthusiasm spread as they made plans. I heard from one of the parents a few months later. Not only was that school yard a glistening success, but they had expanded the Broom Brigade to other schools in the neighborhood as well as to parks, sidewalks, and street corners and had received support from the neighborhood businesses. A community effort bloomed from one small group of determined parents. Their frustration was replaced by pride and success.

I have found that family involvement in schools increases student achievement, parent understanding, and teacher satisfaction. Together, schools can work with parents and families to develop strategies for overcoming barriers to parent involvement.

Schools and teachers can do many things to increase parent involvement, including the following successful practices that I have observed in schools around the country.

- Schools send surveys home (in several languages if necessary) to parents to ask them about their needs for their children, their willingness to participate in school activities, as well as their perceptions of the school.

- Many schools have a parent center or a room just for parents. Coffee, snacks, books, toys for preschoolers, even food coupons and bus schedules can be found there.

- A telephone tree works in some communities, where one parent has to contact only one or two others to pass information along.

- One school takes pictures of the parents with their children at every school event and function. For little or no cost, parents are given the gift of a shared experience and priceless memory. The school has provided a positive reinforcement to the learning experience that will be remembered long after all the popcorn and red punch is forgotten.

- In schools that have successful parental programs and a large population of parents who speak languages other than English, much attention is paid to multiculturalism and to those parents who have limited English skills. Translators, tutors, and someone to answer parents' questions in their own language are always available.

- Programs that involve the children always bring out the parents. Talent shows, plays, concerts, fashion shows, and fairs are tremendously successful.

One school in California I visited put on a talent show. The program was amazing. It was conducted in Spanish, Chinese, Arabic, and English. The children showed mastery not only of their parts in the performance but also of their ability to work together to create a successful show, which is certainly a step to working together in a diverse society. The parents came and learned as well, cheering for the children who, with the help of their teachers, were leading their parents into a new world of understanding. The students were heroes that day. So were their parents, who came to support them.

I visited a class of third graders recently. They were energetic, engaging, and full of questions for me. Finally I decided to asked them a question. "Who do you think is a hero today?"

The room, which had been noisy and full of life, became suddenly and ominously quiet. They thought for a moment, their faces showing consternation with foreheads frowned. One little girl raised her hand. "What's a hero?" she asked.

"A hero is someone, either a man or woman, who stands for goals and ideals that others look up to, someone who is admired and respected, someone who cares for others, someone whose life is worth imitating," I answered carefully, trying to use words that nine-year-olds could understand. I wrote the key words on the board.

They were silent again, thinking hard. It took a long time. Finally, a boy raised his hand. "Michael Jordan," he said with a grin. "I want to be like Mike."

Many of his classmates agreed. "Yeah," they chimed in, "Michael Jordan is our hero."

"Why?" I asked.

"'Cause he can play some ball!" snorted a girl in the back who assumed I ought to know that.

"And he's rich!" asserted another.

"And he don't do drugs!" added another child proudly.

"Yeah, but he retired and all he does now is underwear commercials!" another child commented. They all laughed at that.

"I agree with you," I told them. "Michael is a wonderful role model. Have any of you ever met him?" I asked.

"I saw him play," a tall boy in the front boasted, "in Chicago!" The rest of the class was duly impressed. "But he don't play no more," the boy said sadly.

"That's wonderful," I told him. "But have any of you met him?"

"He don't live around here," they scowled at me.

"Are there any heroes who live around here?" I asked.

"Of course not," they told me, laughing, "nobody lives around here but ordinary people."

"Are any of them heroes?" I asked. "Can an 'ordinary' person be a hero?"

"I guess if he saves somebody from a burning house," a girl suggested.

"What if all he or she does is go to work and live a good life? But what if he or she fits in our definition of hero?" I continued.

They pondered for a moment. "I guess," a girl said thoughtfully, "that my momma could be a hero then. She works real hard and she makes me do my homework. I want to be like her when I grow up," she said quietly.

"Can parents be heroes?" I asked.

"My daddy is strong. He can beat up Mike Tyson!"

"My father always makes sure I got my lunch money."

"My mother lets my friends sleep over."

"My mother is the best cook in the world."

"My grandma is rich 'cause she takes care of me and my five sisters."

Gradually they began to see that parents can indeed be heroes. Just as we provide food when a child is hungry, clothing when a child is cold, even entertainment for diversion, we have a responsibility to provide models and guides for edification, inspiration, and education. Children are thirsty for direction and guidance. Their thirst today is quenched by musicians and actors, by cartoons and video games—thin substances that leave them grounded only to liquid anchors. Good heroes are stabilizers of the spirit; the more inspiring the hero, the more inspired the child. That's the job of adults.

Children today need solidity, strength, and security as they grow and face a world that is sure to be filled with fierce challenges. They need heroes. They need their parents, grandparents, or whatever their family makeup is. They need strong supportive teachers. They need you to be their hero.

As a teacher, I value parents and any assistance they can give me. As a parent, I appreciate teachers and the surrogate parent role they often play. Together, we are a powerful, heroic force that can change the world for the students we both love.

4

Alex Haley, Me, and a Kid Named Kyrus

A Tale of Cosmic Connections

It was January 1977. I watched, fascinated, along with the rest of America, the televised version of Alex Haley's monumental book, *Roots*. Over 130 million people tuned in to watch the story of a slave called Kunta Kinte and how this young man, snatched from his native land and transported in the hold of a slave ship to this country, became the ancestor of a strong family of African Americans, the family of Alex Haley.

I was teaching at a junior high school at the time, and I remember that all the discussions, whether in the teachers' lounge or in the classroom, surrounded that powerful story. The school atmosphere was tense and polarized. The black students felt angry and confrontational, while the white students, who the day before had been their friends, felt guilty and defensive. Class discussions brought out previously unspoken feelings and deeply hidden biases and hurts. Even though the dramatization sought to end each story with a message of hope, it was impossible to escape the realities of slavery, degradation, and human depravity. The film, and the book on which it was based, detailed the horrors of the hold of the slave ship, the shame of the auction block, the pain and confusion of families torn apart, and the realities of forced labor under terrible conditions. But it also showed the unquenchable will to live, the determination to survive and overcome, and the power of the human spirit.

The dramatization of that book changed the lives of all us who witnessed it. Alex Haley became a household name. His family history, and the story of how he had traced his roots back to Africa—a feat rarely accomplished by any black American up to that point—became our own. He awakened an interest in genealogy, particularly among African Americans, and offered them a way finally to reflect on the hideous past of slavery with something close to pride. He helped transpose everyone's view of history. I admired him for his skill, his ability to write and draw a picture with words, as well as his humanity and humility.

Alex Haley was raised on a farm in Henning, Tennessee. As a child, he sat on the wide front porch of the family home, listening to stories from his maternal grandmother, Cynthia Palmer, who traced the family genealogy to Haley's great-great-great-great-grandfather, an African called "Kin-tay," who was brought by slave ship to America. Years later, Haley embarked on an odyssey that took eleven years and is now part of literature history. On the basis of family tradition and his own research, Haley traveled to the village of Juffure, in Gambia, West Africa, to trace his own ancestors. He met with the village *griot*, or oral historian, who could name Haley's own ancestor Kunta Kinte.

The resulting book, *Roots*, was published in 1976 to much critical acclaim. In one year, the book sold more than a million copies, one of which belonged to me.

I cherished that book and all it meant, and kept it in a special place in my bookcase. I used excerpts from the book—and from the videotapes when they were later released—in my classroom. We discussed issues of fairness and racism and bigotry and redemption. We connected the ideas in the book with history lessons as well as with American literature of that period. We read poetry of Paul Dunbar, Claude McKay, and Walt Whitman, as well as Maya Angelou. We read the life of Lincoln and the life of Frederick Douglass. My students devoured the concepts, accepted the challenges, and absorbed the underlying lessons that were offered through this integrated study. It was multicultural, cross-curricular teaching and learning at its best, and I didn't even know it. I just knew they were thriving and enjoying the learning process with no pain and much gain. Alex Haley helped me to do that.

By 1990, I was teaching ninth grade at a junior-senior high school, still focusing on cross-curricular lessons that touched on important concepts and issues. A student once asked me, "Don't you know you're an English teacher? Why you keep givin' us all this history and stuff?"

I just smiled and told him that a piece of literature made no sense unless you could understand its historical context. "You gotta know where the author is coming from," I explained. He looked at me doubtfully, but he truly enjoyed our choral reading of Robert Hayden's poem "Middle Passage" as we began our unit of American literature and history and culture that year, which was always climaxed by excerpts from the videotapes of *Roots*.

A large part of any English classroom is, of course, writing assignments, and I did my best to give meaningful assignments, and even opportunities for students to have their work published in various venues, like the library journal or poetry contests. One day, a student named Jared came to me and handed me a crumpled piece of paper that had been ripped from a magazine. On it was an application for a short story contest. He said to me in that deep, gravelly sounding voice of challenge that only a ninth grader can have, "Here! You think you so bad—why don't YOU write something!"

I looked at him, grinned, and said, "Well, Jared, maybe I'll just do that!" I tossed the application into my bag, along with cut slips, red pens, dozens of paper clips, six books, and three hundred ungraded papers, and forgot about it.

On the way home, I stopped by the grocery store to pick up fixings for dinner, thinking only of whether or not spaghetti sauce was on sale this week. I was pushing my cart down an aisle when a woman came toward me from the other direction. In her cart was a chubby, almost cherubic-looking three-year-old, standing amidst the food items his mother had selected. He was grinning and reaching for her. Instead of reaching for her son, I heard her say to him as she passed me, "If you don't sit your stinkin', useless butt back down in that shopping cart, I swear I'll bust your greasy face in!"

Shocked, I looked at her sharply but said nothing. The child sat down heavily, his smile gone. She rushed past me and headed to the checkout lane. I found the spaghetti sauce and pasta I was looking for, but I was no longer hungry. I couldn't get the face of that child out of my mind. What kind of life must he have at home? If she treats him like this in public, what might she do in private?

When I got to the parking lot of the grocery store, I searched for the child and his mother, but they had vanished. Thinking back, perhaps I should have said something to her. Perhaps I should have followed her out and copied down the license-plate number of her car. To tell whom? The police? Social services? And tell them what? That she yelled at her child? That's not against the law.

I got home and fixed dinner for my family, but I was distracted as we ate. I could not stop thinking about that child. I sat down at my computer, and before I was consciously aware of it, I started writing. In two hours it was finished—only three typed pages—a powerful short story that took that little boy home and saw his life through the eyes of my imagination. (The story, called "One Small Torch," can be found in its entirety in Appendix A.)

I pulled out the application that Jared had given me, filled out the entry form, put the whole thing in an envelope, and sealed it. I grabbed my coat, drove to the post office, and mailed it before I could think about it or change my mind. I was driven purely by emotion, not reason.

The next day I sheepishly told Jared that I had written something for the contest, and we continued with class. Eventually, I forgot about it.

Four months later, I was at home, sitting on my bed grading papers—a dangerous practice because sleep jumps up and grabs you in the middle of a paragraph—when the phone rang, and a deep, cultured voice said, "May I speak to Sharon Draper, please?"

"Speaking."

"I'm from *Ebony* magazine, and I'm in charge of the short story contest. We had thousands of entries, you know."

"I'm glad I didn't have to grade them," I chuckled. "How did I do?"

"I'm pleased to announce that your story, 'One Small Torch,' came in first place!"

"You're kidding! What does that mean?"

"It means your story will be published and very shortly we will be sending you a check for *five thousand dollars!*"

I gasped and screeched and, I think, jumped on the bed, stepping all over graded and ungraded essays on Shakespeare.

When the story was printed, it was as if I had won the Pulitzer Prize. Reporters from the local newspaper asked to interview me. I got my picture, in full color, on the front page of the Tempo section, with a wonderful article on the story and its power and simplicity. I was a little over-whelmed. People started asking me for autographs.

"My autograph?" I asked incredulously. "I don't know how to sign an autograph! I sign detention slips!"

I got letters from people from all over the country, people who had read the story and were touched by it. I was amazed. But the most amazing and most treasured letter came in early 1991. On his own letterhead paper, written in his own handwriting, was a letter from someone I would never in a million years expect to hear from. It said,

Dear Sharon M. Draper,

I read your story and I think it is wonderful. You have written a most graphically dramatic story. It rings with an authenticity that makes a reader chill. . . . You are a skilled writer and have much to offer. Keep up the good work.

Brotherly love,

Alex Haley

I trembled as I read it. I could not believe that the person I so admired, a writer I so respected, would take the time from his busy schedule to offer words of encouragement to me. He called me a writer! It was the first time that I even entertained the notion of being a "writer." I knew I was a teacher. I knew I was pretty good at editing student writing, but it never occurred to me that I, too, could be a writer.

I took the letter to school and showed my students and colleagues, who were properly awed. Jared, the student who had started the whole process, had moved to another state, and I was never able to track him down and thank him, but the rest of my students and I celebrated with pizza and pop and, knowing me, probably a little poetry.

But the story doesn't end there. Alex Haley died on February 10, 1992, just a year after he sent me that letter, and I was truly saddened. Not only was a great and generous man gone forever, but a voice in the darkness was forever silenced.

I continued to teach, using Alex Haley's words, his spirit, and his ability to inspire in my lesson planning and in my life. I decided to try to write a book and was unbelievably successful with my first attempt, *Tears of a Tiger*. When it was time for the sequel, which is called *Forged by Fire*, I decided to use the short story that started it all, "One Small Torch," as the first chapter. *Forged by Fire* went on to win the Coretta Scott King Award and numerous other awards for literature for young people. At the award ceremony, I took special pains to mention Alex Haley and how influential he had been on my life.

Twenty-three years after the showing of *Roots* on television, nine years after I received the letter from Alex Haley, and three years after the publication of *Forged by Fire*, I sat in the back seat of a car, heading down the sunny roads of Tennessee toward the little town of Clinton and Alex Haley's farm, which he built when he became a successful writer. I was giddy with excitement. Of course, the farm now belonged to the Children's Defense Fund, but many of the original buildings remained, and I knew that Alex Haley's spirit walked those lanes and breathed peacefully in the air of the library that had been built there.

The purpose of my visit was to speak to a group of young people who had read *Forged by Fire* during their stay there and who wanted to hear from the author. These young people were special—not the top of their class or the children usually picked for special events like this one. These kids were difficult, troubled, needy in mind and spirit, and on the edge—just about ready to fall off, drop out, give up. They were brought there to build up their spirits, to repair their damaged self-esteem, to find hope and possibilities. The only attention that these tenth graders had ever received in school was negative attention. In just a few days, like wilted daisies that simply needed a little water, I saw them blossom, bloom, and grow under the nurturing attention of the staff. They were given encouragement for once in their lives; they were given goals and responsibilities. It was amazing to see them change as they received something that we assume all young people receive, but unfortunately, too many of them grow to maturity without—positive reinforcement and love.

On the last day, they marched in proudly for the graduation ceremonies. They sang, they hugged, they wept. I spoke to them about dreams and rainbows and golden possibilities, which can be found in spite of the harsh realities of many of their lives. I told them of Alex Haley and how he had influenced my life and how, even long after his death, he touched and inspired all of us. I charged them with heading out into the future with heads held high, and they cheered loud and long.

After the ceremony, we proceeded to that wide, welcoming porch, exactly like the one where, long ago, Alex's grandmother told him those stories about the captured slave, and I signed copies of my books, which had been inspired by his spirit. It was humbling and awesome.

I was almost finished when a young man approached me. He was long and gangly and had eyes that had seen pain, though he wore a grin on his face. His name was Kyrus.

"You got any more of them *Tears of a Tiger* books?"

"I'm sorry, they're all gone," I replied with regret. I had brought a few books with me, and stupidly forgetting how powerful a good book can be in the hands of a child who needs it, I had not brought enough. I had just given away the last one.

"I ain't never read no book before—not all the way through. But your book was good. I couldn't put it down. My moms couldn't believe it—'cause I was readin'. I read *Forged by Fire* in one night."

"I'll be glad to sign *Forged by Fire* for you, but we've run out of *Tears of a Tiger*. I'm really sorry."

"Oh, that's OK. Just write down the title. I don't hardly ever go to the library, but I'm gonna go to the library as soon as I get home and see if I can find it. I just gotta read that book!"

Now I actually did have one copy left of *Tears of a Tiger*. It was the copy I used when I gave presentations, and it was battered and torn and dirty, with markings all through it. It was in the bottom of my purse. I dug down and pulled it out slowly.

"This is my own copy, and it's a little beat up, but if you want it, you can have it."

"For real? Oh, I can?"

"It's yours," I said gently. I wrote "For my friend Kyrus—may all your dreams come true" on the front page and signed my name. He was almost dancing with excitement. I was near tears.

"I'm gonna read this on the plane," he said. "I bet I'll have it finished before I get home. Wait till I show my moms! Thank you so much!"

I handed him the book and he bounded off the porch in two steps, crowing to his friends in exultation that he'd received the very last copy of *Tears of a Tiger*. He clutched the book to him like it was the Holy Grail. Maybe, in a sense, it was. I could feel the presence of Alex Haley smiling broadly. Thank you, Kyrus. Thank you, Alex Haley. Thank you so much.

5

Reach Out and Touch,
If You Can

Observations, Assumptions, and
Flexibility

I love visiting schools. The raw square architecture, the heavy doors at the front entrance—sometimes too heavy to pull open with one hand. I'm not sure why school doors are designed so. It seems to me that the doors to education should move smoothly and easily on well-oiled hinges, beckoning the student to the place where knowledge awaits. But I know the reality. They are heavy, often bolted with steel bars, often alarmed and armored as if prepared for invasion. Metal detectors, even in the best suburban schools, stand like fierce centurions in homage to our society of fear and violence.

Once inside, the hallways always have that smell of expectation and French fries and adolescent excitement. To the left is the main office where sits an astute secretary who knows every student and every teacher, as well as all their secrets. She types, answers the phone, hands out tissues and Band-Aids, and knows the schedule of every single human in the building.

Turn the corner and the same hallway appears in every single school. It is long, with classrooms plugged into it like kindergarten building blocks. Student drawings, writing, or creative expression grace the walls. If it is an elementary school, there are colorful pictures of butterflies or birds with the name of each child printed neatly below, to show who is special in Room 101. Their names, unique little sparks of creativity, that reflect parents' need to show their child their remarkable place in the world. Unusual names like Europa or Boquisha or Metamorphosis. Strong, stable names like James or Charles or Robert. Modern suburban names like Heather or Chelsea or Madison. Each one a bright spark of hope and possibility.

If it is a high school, names on construction paper have been replaced by miles of numbered lockers reflecting the sameness and institutionalization of schools. Always made of sturdy metal, sometimes painted in pastel colors, the lockers are temporary storage spaces for books and pencils and coats and lost homework and misplaced dreams.

A glance into a classroom shows the teacher walking around the class wearing comfortable shoes, washable clothes, and a smile. That teacher cajoles, pleads, jokes, grins, encourages, emotes, and shares. Sometimes there is a flash of electricity and learning has occurred.

Teachers are the most flexible humans on the face of the earth. They know that all lesson plans are contingency plans, that their completion depends upon thousands of other factors besides the teacher and the student. The school day, filled with hundreds of children who have individual needs and requirements, is a constant ebb and flow of what we plan to do and what we actually accomplish.

Meetings called. Meetings canceled. Meetings with parents, principals, the PTA, and the retirement specialist who shows up once a year just to tease. Interruptions to the classroom for important things like student schedule changes and for minor details like tornadoes and hurricanes. There's a dog in the hall. A fire drill. A real fire. An assembly. A pep rally. An observer to your classroom from someone in the central office, who obviously knows nothing about reality because she wears spiked heels and a silk suit.

It's time for making out next year's schedules, passing out report cards and bus cards. It's time for surveys—on safety, on drugs in the classroom, on student opinions.

Because we are required to do so, we administer standardized tests, which, if we are successful, prove to someone at the state department that the students know what's on the test. Not that they are educated or well learned, or even intelligent. Just that they know what is on the test. What else matters?

I wonder how well the students of Socrates would have done on some of these tests. Confucius once said, "Learning without thought is useless, but thought without learning is dangerous." How are we to do both? Are we to produce adults who can think and reason and make logical leaps of wisdom, or are we to produce people who can answer questions on a test? Because we are more flexible than the granite-minded creators of standardized learning, we constantly strive to do both—create young people who can think as well as respond correctly to a given stimulus.

This ability to be flexible even transfers to our personal lives. We are less likely to be upset when a favorite TV show is canceled or when an item we want at the hardware store is out of stock because we live with cancellations and shortages all the time. We appreciate repair people who arrive at our homes on time and drug stores that stay open all night. When problems arise, we are able to adjust with equanimity to almost any situation.

Once, while staying in a city in the West, I had a conversation that might have really ticked off someone who had not taught for almost thirty years. But while I can cope with anything—I teach—this one stretched even my patience and flexibility. I was in my hotel room and I needed a wake-up call. I called the front desk.

"Hello, this is the Plaza Hotel. May I help you?"

"This is Sharon Draper, Room 428, and I . . ."

Click. Ring. Machine Voice. "The party in Room 428 is not available. Please leave a message. . . ."

I tried the front desk again.

"Hello, this is the Plaza Hotel. May I help you?"

"Yes, this is Sharon Draper, and I . . ."

"Oh, Miss Draper, you just had a call. You just missed it."

"That was me who just called."

"You called yourself?"

"No, I called you, and I want to tell you that . . ."

"One moment, please."

She put me on hold. I listened to tinny telephone music. After five minutes, she returned.

"Hello, this is the Plaza Hotel. May I help you?"

"Yes. My name is Sharon Draper, and I . . ."

"You certainly are popular today. This is the third call you've received in five minutes! Let me put you through to your voice mail."

"No, wait!" I tried to stop her, but she clicked off. Once again I heard the mechanical message.

"The party in Room 428 is not available. Please leave a message. . . ."

I tried once more. The same cheerful voice answered.

"Hello, this is the Plaza Hotel. May I help you?"

"Listen carefully," I said. "My name is Sharon Draper. I am a guest in this hotel. I would like a six o'clock wake-up call."

"Let me connect you to reservations. One moment, please."

"Wait! I just want a wake-up call!" It was too late. She had transferred me to another desk.

"Hello, this is the Plaza Hotel. May I help you?" the male voice said officiously.

"Is this the reservations desk?" I asked.

"One moment." He was gone in a second. The tinny telephone music was on a loop. I was back to their version of "Moon River."

"Kitchen. Jeff speaking."

"I'm trying to reach the reservations desk."

"You want dinner reservations. Let me transfer you to the restaurant."

"No! Wait!" I was back to the shores of "Moon River."

"Dining Room."

"I'm trying to reach the reservations desk."

"This is reservations. What time would you like dinner, and how many are in your party?"

"I don't want dinner. I just want a six o'clock wake-up call."

"I'm sorry, ma'am, but the restaurant doesn't open until noon. You could order room service at 6:00 A.M. if you like."

"I'm not hungry. I just want to wake up on time."

"Let me transfer you to the front desk. They handle those requests. Why would you call the restaurant for a wake-up call?" He sounded annoyed. "Moon River" returned.

"Hello, this is the Plaza Hotel. May I help you?"

"This is room 428. I would like a six o'clock wake-up call tomorrow, PLEASE!"

"A.M. or P.M.?"

"A.M."

She hesitated. Then she said, and I swear that this is true, "Ma'am, could you call back about five in the morning? The lady who does wake-up calls won't be in until then."

"Sure, no problem. Why not? I give up!"

"Good night, ma'am, and thanks for calling the Plaza Hotel!"

Teachers face that kind of thinking all the time. In order to deal with the bureaucracy of the central office or the state board of education, they often must adjust to frustrating situations. The teacher, for example, who was told to stop teaching the book *Old Yeller* because it showed cruelty to animals and the word "yellow" was spelled incorrectly. Or the teacher who had to buy her own classroom supplies and was not reimbursed because she bought red pencils for her students instead of the required school color, which was blue. Or the teacher who started in September to fill out forms in duplicate and triplicate and to get them countersigned and authorized for supplies he needed in December. The materials arrived the day after school let out in June.

But in spite of the difficulties, schools always make me feel refreshed and revitalized because of the internal elasticity of young people. When the bell rings and the halls become instantly crowded with students, their individuality becomes homogenized with their desperate need for conformity. Whether they wear uniforms or not, they will have the same hair styles, makeup, or jewelry. If it is a school where rules about appearance are relaxed, they will strive so hard to be outrageous that their body piercings and tattoos will manage to reach a level of peer conformity. If it is a school where rules about appearance are stringent, minor challenges such as rolled socks or red nail polish seek to mock the status quo—but all of them do it, thus eliminating the challenge. They seek their own private voice, which they scream individually to the universe. It joins all the rest of the private voices and becomes a chorus.

I once spoke at a suburban junior high school in a Midwestern county that had seen much change in the past twenty years. The school had once been the center of a huge farming district. Children of farmers, who worked with their families, married each other, and then became farmers themselves, had been the backbone of the school for generations. They were comfortable with each other and proud of their agrarian background.

But slowly, as farming became more difficult and less lucrative, as farms began to fold and families began to disperse, the county became less agrarian and more suburban. Huge plots of farmland were bought and slowly turned into housing developments and malls and industrial parks. Fast-food places replaced roadside stands, and many local merchants were forced out of business by huge hardware and department stores. Urban flight and upward mobility made what used to be farm country prime retail land.

This school underwent a vast change. Traditions were discarded for newer standards. The annual Cornhuskers Ball was replaced by the June Jazz Jam. Home economics and woodworking and shop classes were phased out of the curriculum. The school became an odd collection of children from very different backgrounds.

Everyone had to adjust, to be flexible, and to adapt to the changing school dynamics. The teachers, many of whom represented the generation of former farmers, and many of whom represented the newer influx of students, were used to it. The students, however, had more difficulty.

It seemed to me that the school population consisted of three groups—the Ustabees, the Wannabees, and three black girls. Of course they didn't call themselves by these names, and neither did I, but it was clear what their needs were. The Ustabees were the children of the farmers, those families determined to hold on, in spite of the fact that huge farms in South America were now producing what they no longer could.

What was once farmland now became subdivisions where the Wannabees had moved in. The Wannabees were the children of prosperous doctors and lawyers and other professionals. They all had cell phones and drove sports cars. They had taken way too much soccer and gymnastics and organized sports at much too young an age. They were the children of modern suburbia—driven, prosperous, successful. These were the children who were pushed, the children who never learned how to just play because they were never allowed to. They were, however, masters at playing the game of prosperous desperation their parents played so well.

The Ustabees, the children of what used to be called the "good old boys," embrace their parents' philosophy but hide it behind brand-name shirts and shoes, behind a casual acceptance of the newcomers' attitudes and standards. The two groups didn't like each other much, but each knew the difference and didn't cross the line. Despite their cultural differences, there was an unspoken similarity that gave them a measure of comfort with each other: They were all white. This school had no Asian students and no cross-cultural students—except for three black girls.

My heart wept for them. They were the only African American children in the whole school, the only children that were not part of the dominant culture. Those children of former farmers and future corporation presidents had at least a common racial background. But these three girls had only each other.

They came to me after my presentation and said, "Can we talk to you?" They wanted a cure for racism in ten minutes. "Can you give us any advice?" they asked. "How do we deal with all these kids who don't want us here?" They wanted me to tell them how to cope, how to deal with the daily small indignities—the words, the smirks, the feeling in the air, the things that could not be reported to the principal.

One, whose name was Makeba, invited controversy and got it in large doses. She dressed in African garb, questioned every fact from her American History book for cultural relevance, and made inflammatory statements whenever she had the opportunity. She said, "As long as I'm going to be here, they're going to learn something from me!

The other two, Liz and Jackie, just wanted to fit in, be accepted, and not have to fight. Liz was shy and thin, her face full of teenage acne. She would have had trouble being a teenager in any situation. Her friend Jackie was delightful and personable, a young woman who, in perhaps another school situation, might have been the prom queen or the president of student council. She had tried out for cheerleader and had not been chosen. She had run for class office and had not been selected. She had even been discouraged from being in the modeling club. For young women who had enough to deal with simply by being fifteen, their social situation was almost unbearable.

I told them their parents had moved out to the suburbs to give them a better life and did not realize what they were putting their kids through. I told them I could not change 1,500 kids in that school and neither could they.

I asked them if they had any white friends and they said yes. So I told them to cherish and nurture those friendships and keep themselves isolated from the mass of hatred because they could not fight it or change it. I wished I could have given them more. I told them to read *Warriors Don't Cry* by Melba Patillo Beals. It's a firsthand account of the Arkansas nine who integrated Little Rock High School in 1957. The girls, of course, had never heard of Little Rock, but they were intrigued. Such a small pebble to offer children who needed a mountain.

They found that mountain in one of their teachers, who had joined our conversation. She was young, energetic, and seemed to care about all of her students. She was also honest. She knew about flexibility and that the students in that school would have to learn the flexibility of teachers because those three students would next year be joined by ten more, then fifty more, then hundreds, if prevailing social trends continue.

"I'll help you," she said to the students.

Makeba was instantly wary. "How?" she asked sullenly. Jackie and Liz, grateful for straws, looked hopeful.

"Let's start a social diversity project. Let's plan activities that will take us out into the community. Let's do something for other people—folks who are less fortunate than we are. Perhaps it will start a cycle of understanding. What do you think?" she asked them. "Got any ideas?"

"Is it just us, or the other kids too?" asked Jackie.

"Whoever wants to be involved," the teacher replied emphatically.

"Can we collect toys for the Free Store?" Liz wanted to know.

"How about old people? My grandma is old and she loves company. We can maybe visit them," Jackie suggested.

The teacher told them enthusiastically that all their ideas were wonderful, and that they would have a meeting the next day for all interested students.

"Maybe the way to get these kids together is to get them involved in something outside of their lives, something bigger than they are," she told me later. "They've got to learn to be flexible and to adjust to a changing world. But don't worry—I'll be here to help."

I smiled as I left their school. They would make it.

6

Burned Out, Beat Up, and Torn Down

The Story of Rosa

My friend Rosa trudged to school each day with a sigh and a smile. She loved her job at the large urban high school where she taught American History. She loved the interaction with her students, the attention to detail that the study of history offered, and best of all, the times when the class veered "off the subject" into discussions of current social situations or political problems. But, like all of us, she hated the mindless paperwork, the weakened curriculum, and the meaningless details that threatened to overwhelm her joy of teaching. She also worried that the harder she tried, the less effect her efforts were having on her students. Often it seemed they rarely listened and really didn't care whether they learned at all.

She had been teaching fifteen years—long enough to be comfortable in what she did, long enough to know she would never switch to another profession, but not long enough to see retirement as anything but a faint haze on a distant horizon. She had seen classes grow more crowded, her students more needy—for love as well as instruction—and her classroom goals more frustratingly impossible to reach. The administration, helplessly tied by state regulations and lack of funding, valiantly tried to maintain order in a system that was not working very well for students or teachers.

But Rosa kept trying. She wasn't always sure why, but she kept trying. She spent her own money on supplies for children who could not afford them, for supplementary books for them to read, for posters and planters to decorate her room. She gave up lots of her own time, staying after school to encourage a student who was struggling academically or socially, giving up her lunch period to tutor, and coming in early to prepare lively, interesting lessons. But her efforts often seemed meaningless and unsatisfying.

She shared her frustration with me one Saturday when we met for lunch and a movie, a necessary diversion that we sometimes took from the stresses of the week.

"I don't know if I'm doing any good," she told me.

"The kids love you," I said.

"They tolerate me. There's a difference," she retorted as she sipped her diet soda.

"They show up!" I teased, trying to make her laugh. "Every day! Even snow days!"

"Sometimes I wish they wouldn't!" she tossed back.

"They know you care about them. They know your heart is in the right place," I told her gently.

"Yeah, but they'd love to see my heart on a platter!" she retorted.

"Not true! They come back to visit you. That's always a good sign. Even the ones who you thought you hadn't reached," I reminded her.

"They just want to see if I've given up and gone home for good, or if I'm dead yet," she chuckled.

The following Thursday Rosa began third bell with attendance as usual. Jackie, a large girl with a generally nasty attitude, came into class ten minutes late. Rosa asked for a tardy slip.

"I ain't got no tardy slip!"

"It's usually a good idea to have one when you're this late to class," Rosa reminded her quietly.

"You ought to be glad I showed up!" Jackie said, mumbling curse words under her breath.

"Actually, I am. Please take your seat. And bring a note next time." Rosa decided that a confrontation this early in the morning was not worth the effort. Jackie flounced to her seat and proceeded to take her portable CD player and her earphones out of her book bag, which contained no books.

"Jackie, please put away the earphones. Open your book to page 98."

Jackie ignored her.

Rosa said louder, "Jackie, please put away the earphones. We're discussing slavery just before the Civil War. Please open your book to page 98."

Jackie looked up, sneered, and began to sing along with the CD.

Rosa said once more, "Jackie, put those earphones away right this minute. Unless that's a CD of the Civil War, it's not the time or place for music."

Jackie rolled her eyes and slowly removed the earphones. She did not bother to look for her book, but she was quiet, for the moment. Rosa told me all of this weeks later, but I know her well enough to know how the class went on that day.

Rosa continued with class, leading the students into a discussion of the social issues surrounding slavery. Most of the class were animated and interested in the subject because it was controversial, raised sensitive issues, and allowed them to talk and share instead of listen and take notes.

"Why didn't the slaves just leave?" asked Malcolm.

"Many tried," Rosa offered, giving the class just enough to continue the discussion.

"It's hard to hide when you're black and the whole world is white," commented Rufus, who was usually loud and outspoken.

"Yeah, but when they got caught, they got beaten or maimed, or whipped," Lucinda reminded them.

"Or sold," said Fred.

"Or their family sold," added Thelma.

"Intimidation mixed with fear and pain are powerful weapons," Rosa offered.

"How can one person own another person anyway?" asked LaQuinta.

"Slavery is not an American idea. There was slavery in Ancient Rome," Rosa told the class.

"I think it's barbaric that humans do that to each other," said Jeff, an honor student.

"Your mama was a slave!" This was from Jackie, who had listened silently and sullenly throughout the discussion.

"That was unnecessary!" Rosa chided Jackie. "If you can't add anything positive to the discussion, then just say nothing."

"You can't shut me up!" roared Jackie. "I got a right to say what I think, and I say your greasy, stinky mama was a slave and loved it when white men raped her!"

Rosa, surprised by the violence of Jackie's outburst, walked toward her to say something to perhaps calm her down. She never made it to the back of the room where Jackie sat, for Jackie stood quickly, picked up her desk, lifted it over her head, and hurled it with all of her strength at Rosa.

The desk hit Rosa with full force. The chair part of the desk struck Rosa on her head while the legs connected with her chest. She fell to the floor in an unconscious heap, the desk still covering her body.

The students in the class, stunned for a moment, did not know what to do. Some of the girls screamed. Some ran into the hall calling for help. Jackie left in the confusion, and no one tried to stop her. Jeff took off his jacket and covered Rosa's unconscious body. LaQuinta called the office on the intercom and told them to call 911. Fred made all of the students except for Lucinda and Jeff leave the room and sit in the hall. Malcolm took charge of the class in the hall and kept them calm and quiet. LaQuinta gave everyone Kleenex if they were crying and offered candy from her book bag.

The life squad arrived quickly and Rosa, still unconscious and bleeding from a gash on her head, was taken from the school and rushed to a nearby hospital. News reporters showed up at the school shortly after, anxious to report a vicious act of violence in a public school. Police cars lined the school parking lot, and school was finally dismissed early by the principal. Jackie was located and arrested.

I went to see Rosa in the hospital the next day. She was severely bruised and had a deep gash on her head. While she was not as seriously hurt as I feared, she would still be out of school for several weeks. But her spirit had been badly damaged.

"I'm never going back," she told me.

"Why not?" I asked gently.

"They hate me, and it's not worth it."

"They do not hate you," I said firmly. "Look at all the cards and flowers. They are all from your students—even students from years ago."

"Next time, one of them is going to shoot me," she said, ignoring me.

"Did you know that Jackie had been raped by a gang of boys the night before she attacked you?"

Rose looked up in surprise. "And she came to school?" In spite of herself, her attention, and her concern, was turned to her students—even the one who had attacked her.

"She didn't hate you. She was suffering, and you were simply the one who was available to vent her pain and anger and shame upon. That doesn't make it right, but at least there's an explanation."

Rosa sighed and leaned back into her pillow.

"Do you know how you got to the hospital?" I asked her.

"I don't remember anything."

"Your students. The ones you said don't care. The ones you think you don't make a difference with. They called 911. They kept you warm. They kept you safe. They covered you with their own clothes. They sat here in the hospital in the waiting room all night long. They're still down there. They love you, Rosa."

I picked up a few of the cards that had accumulated on the table next to her bed.

"Let me read a couple of these to you," I suggested. She nodded in assent.

"Here's one from Lucinda. She made it herself. It says, 'I'm sorry I ever thought bad things about you while I was doing my homework. You're a really good teacher, even if you are a little hard, and I hope you come back soon.'"

Rosa smiled a little.

"Here's another. It's from Fred. Looks like he spent all his lunch money for a week on this card. The flowery preprinted message is nice, but look what he wrote at the bottom. 'I miss your smile and your stupid red pen. Please get well quick so you can use that red pen on me again. I need it. All of us do. Love, Fred.'"

"Here's a card from LaQuinta. 'When you get back all the girls want to take you shopping. You could use some cute shoes. We love you and we miss you.'"

Rosa blinked back tears. "I had no idea."

"When you're all healed up and feeling better, remember that those kids need you. It's easy to focus on one student who was awful and violent and terrible. And it's easy to forget the thirty-two other students who worried about you and cared for you. You have to go back for them. They love you and they need you. And I think you need them too."

After a lengthy recuperation, Rosa did decide to return to the classroom. Her students made welcome-back signs and decorated the room with flowers. She glanced around them, gave each of them a hug, and said, "Let's get started. Open your books. We have a lot to learn."

7

Turning Rocks into Rubies

The Lesson of the Stones

A s teachers we tread upon a rocky path. Pebbles of limitations, restrictions, and regulations get between our toes, stones of apathy, failure, and futility trip us and make us fall, and huge boulders of violence, prejudice, and inequity block the path completely, making some of us sit down and give up or turn around and go in the other direction. But the same pebbles and stones that cause one person to fall can be used by another to build a great cathedral. The boulders that cause one person to fail can be used by another to build a bridge. When we see a pile of rocks on our path, do we see an impassible mountain, or the possibility of what those rocks can be?

Antoine de Saint-Exupery, the author of *The Little Prince*, says, "A rock pile ceases to be a rock pile the moment a single man contemplates it, bearing within him the image of a cathedral." We as teachers see cathedrals in each little pile of rocks that sit before us each day. We can visualize the possibilities because we must. Remember the story called "Stone Soup"? What could have been a story of starvation became a wonderful meal because of the creativity and vision of the cook.

If our goal is to create soup from stones and build cathedrals from pebbles—or simply to get to the end of the day, to the end of the week, to spring break, to June, or to retirement—then our goal of getting there and dealing with the problems that confront us is at least as important as the journey.

There are no right answers, no way of knowing whether the choices we make are right or wrong. Our students depend on us, not only to guide them along the rocky path, but also to show them how to build their own cathedrals or their own soup from the rocks and stones strewn in their way. They need us to be the master builders, the master chefs—they need our guidance and instruction, our intervention and understanding.

Tariq was one such young man. He was in the seventh grade. He stopped by my desk one day, just before the bell rang, a serious look on his face.

"I just want to let you know I don't have my homework today," he said.

"You miss quite a bit of homework," I commented in my best teacher voice.

"I know. I can't help it."

"What's the problem?" I asked.

He was hesitant to respond. "I spent the night in the bathtub," he said finally.

I was confused. "Why would you need to take a bath all night?" I asked.

"I wasn't taking a bath," he said, looking at me as if I were stupid. "I was hiding. Mama says that when the shooting gets really bad, the safest place to hide is in the bathtub. She made me stay there all night."

I was stunned. I knew he lived in a rough neighborhood, and I knew that drive-by shootings were common, but it never occurred to me that gunfire could be so bad in an apartment complex that a mother would have to hide her son in the bathtub for safety. I didn't know what to say. I told him to turn his homework in as soon as "things settled down." He thanked me and found his seat in the third row.

The world our students live in is often one that we cannot even imagine. We make assumptions about them and requirements of them that might be impossible for them to accomplish, through no fault of their own. Their road is made of very sharp stones, and we have no shoes to offer them for protection.

Although I guess I shouldn't have been, I was truly surprised when I ran into Tariq not long ago at a local university where I was invited to speak. He was in his third year, doing quite well, majoring in poetry and creative writing. He had found a way to tread lightly on his path.

Sometimes, young people do not want to deal with the problems. They want an easy way out. They remind me of a fictional story about a young man who wanted to breeze by on the path of life with no obstacles, no rocks, no hindrances at all. He wanted to get all of his learning in one fell swoop. This young man was in a hurry, as are many young people. He did not have time to stop for instruction. He didn't have time to consider philosophical questions about the essence of rocks. He wanted to know it all and he wanted it right away.

"Where can I find out everything I need to know in a hurry?" he asked his parents. "I don't have time to sit in a classroom for the rest of my life. I don't have time to be bothered with stumbling and falling."

"What's your hurry?" they responded. "Take your time to learn. Sometimes the rocks are placed in our path for a reason."

The young man brushed past them and went to his teacher. "Where can I find out everything I need to know in a hurry? School takes too long and is too complicated. Isn't there someplace I can go to find out everything right now?"

His teacher responded, "Take your time, son. The path and the rocks are there for a reason. But I don't know all the answers. Go and ask the school librarian."

The young man brushed the teacher aside without a word of thanks and rushed to the school library. "Where can I find out everything I need to know in a hurry?" he asked the librarian.

"What's your hurry?" she asked him. "I suppose you can start by reading all the books we have here. There's certainly a lot of knowledge shelved here."

"That would take too long," the young man replied. "I know that there is an easier, shorter way to find out everything I need to know."

The librarian frowned and replied, "Why don't you ask the principal? He probably knows more than I do. Maybe he knows the answer to what you seek."

The young man brushed the librarian aside without a word of thanks and rushed to the principal's office. "Where can I find out everything I need to know in a hurry? School takes too long and is too complicated. Isn't there someplace I can go to find out everything right now?" he asked the principal impatiently.

The principal pondered a moment, then replied, "Well, I have heard of a place that may or may not really exist, but if it does, the way is long and dangerous, and there are no guarantees. Knowledge such as you seek is a great treasure and is guarded by a dragon that is said to be fierce and deadly."

"I don't care!" the young man declared. "If it will get me out of here with all I need to know in a hurry, then that is what I want. Tell me how to get there."

The principal said to the young man, "If you must go, then you must. The dragon that guards all wisdom and knowledge lives at the top of the highest mountain.

The road is full of rocks and thorns and obstacles. Are you
sure this is what you want to do?"

The young man fiercely insisted that it was, so he
marched from the principal's office and headed to the top of
the mountain to meet the dragon who guarded all knowledge. It was as the principal had said—the road was steep
with jagged boulders that cut the young man's hands and
feet as he climbed. The air became very thin as he neared
the top, but he refused to give up, refused to turn away from
his search to find all knowledge in a hurry.

When he finally reached the top of the mountain, the
young man knocked on the door of the castle he found
there. A huge metallic-red dragon answered the door, fire
and smoke spewing from his mouth.

"What do you want?" the dragon roared.

"I have been told that you hold all knowledge, that you
are the keeper of everything I need to know. School takes
too long and is too complicated. I want to know everything
and I want to know it now!"

The dragon stared at the young man, decided not to
incinerate him for his impudence and arrogance, and finally
said, "I will agree to help you find that knowledge."

The young man started to interrupt. "But . . ."

"Silence!" the dragon roared. "Do you want the knowledge or not?"

"Yes, I really do," the young man answered.

"Then you must do exactly as I say," the dragon continued. "First you must go back down the mountain. . . ."

"But I just got up here!" the young man cried in dismay.

"Do you want the knowledge or not?" the dragon
roared.

"Yes, sir," the young man replied, but he was very dis-
appointed at this turn of events.

"As I was saying," the dragon continued, "first you must
go back down the mountain, then you must go to the banks

of the river. There you will find rocks and stones. Gather as many as you can. Return to me at your convenience and remember that my fee is one rock and one stone."

The young man gasped in disbelief. "You mean I came all the way up here and you send me down the mountain to get some stupid rocks? This has been a complete waste of my time!" The dragon ignored him and closed the door.

The young man trudged back down the mountain to the river. It was getting dark and huge torrents of rain had begun to fall. The young man was soaked by the storm and his feet sank in the mud by the river. Hundreds of rocks and stones littered the riverside, but the young man, angry, wet, and tired, picked up a rock and a stone, stuffed them into the pockets of his jeans, and headed to his home.

The next morning, as the young man lifted his jeans off the back of the chair where he had slung them before he slept, the rock and the stone fell out of the pockets and glittered on the floor in the morning sunlight. The young man blinked, picked them up and examined them with growing excitement. The rock had turned into a ruby and the stone had magically become a diamond. "I'm rich!" the young man gloated. "I'm rich!"

He ran out of his house, precious jewels in hand, and ran back to the mountain. This trip up the mountain took only half the time, for the young man's feet were light with joy and exultation. He reached the home of the dragon, knocked on the door, and when the dragon answered, the young man cried, "Why didn't you tell me the rocks were magic? This is all the knowledge I'll need! I'm rich! I'm rich! I'm rich!"

The dragon looked unimpressed. "I am glad that you are pleased," he said regally. "I will take my fee now." With that, he snatched the ruby and the diamond from the hands of the suddenly confused young man.

"You can't take my riches! They're mine! I found them!" the young man protested.

"I told you my fee was one rock and one stone. These will do," the dragon replied coolly. "You may keep all the others you collected, however." The dragon then tossed the diamond and the ruby on a huge pile of jewels just inside his door, a pile that the young man had failed to notice on his first trip to visit the dragon.

"But I only got those two," the young man replied sadly. "It was dark and cold and wet and I didn't feel like walking in the mud."

"Too bad," the dragon replied.

"But you told me you'd give me all the knowledge in the world!" the young man pleaded.

"You just learned everything you need to know to make it in life," the dragon replied coldly, as he shut and locked his door.

The young man trudged slowly back down the mountain. He went back to the river, but it had rained all night, and the river had overflowed, and the place where the magic rocks and stones had lain was gone forever.

Sometimes the things we see as obstacles, as rocks in our path, are really opportunities, treasures in disguise. There is no easy path to success, no one right way to stack the stones. It is the journey that makes the difference. That is what we must teach our children, and that is what we must also learn.

So I salute all of those who take the journey. All of us who not only show the children the mountain of teaching and learning, but take them by the hand and guide them gently up the mountainous path to knowledge. I salute all who undertake the stony path to success with children:

- The primary teachers who wipe noses, give hugs, and give the children that all-important start in reading and math and in how to live in a community of disparate individuals.

- The middle school teachers who must deal with raging hormones, adolescent overdrive, and the latest rage on MTV.
- The high school teachers who reach out and grab our developing young men and women to give them one last boost of knowledge before adulthood, who know that even at graduation, there is so much more that these young people need to learn.
- The librarians, bus drivers, counselors, secretaries, and custodians, who provide the support services needed to make our schools safe and meaningful.
- The substitutes, without whom we could not take a day off—ever!
- The art teachers and gym teachers and music teachers, who round out the lives of students with beauty and motion.
- The older teachers—the experienced ones who know exactly how many months, weeks, days, and hours they have until retirement, and exactly how much money they will get each month.
- The young teachers—the preservice and beginning teachers who are just starting out and still have the energy and enthusiasm that many of us have lost.

I met a wonderfully talented young man recently who had won several major awards for his writing ability. When I asked him what his career plans were, he said, "Well, I'm going to write books, plays, and poetry. I'm going to win a Pulitzer Prize!"

I admired his enthusiasm and his vision. "So what will you do while you're waiting for the Pulitzer Prize?" I asked.

"Well, I guess I'll teach or something to support myself," he said, with a shrug of his shoulders.

I found myself grinding my teeth and making fists. I spoke slowly and forced a smile. "Let's chat a bit," I said pleasantly. "Teaching is a passion, a vision, a calling to answer a need. You can't do it just because it's something to do."

"Why not?" he asked.

"You know how you feel about your writing?" I asked him. "The deep, passionate, all-consuming desire?" He nodded. "That's how you should feel about teaching!"

"Yeah, but who would ever want to be a teacher?" he countered. "A teacher makes no money, gets no respect, and makes no difference to anyone!"

"Now wait a minute," I told him. "Is this true? Listen to your heart, and remember."

"Remember what?" he asked.

"Which teacher most influenced you?" I asked.

He answered immediately. "Miss Markham—she made me love to write!"

"And if Miss Markham had decided just to 'teach or something,' would she have been your inspiration?"

"No," he admitted.

I told him, "You have the ability to make a difference in the lives of children as yet unborn, by your skill as a writer and poet. If you're going to teach, do it well. Share your gift with the young ones. Become someone's inspiration. Become someone's memory!"

We need young teachers because our generation is about to retire. Who will teach the children when we are gone? Who will light the way upon the rocky path?

I don't know if he took me up on my suggestion, but I feel that I at least removed a stone from his path, and perhaps from the paths of students as yet unborn that he might teach—a stone that he didn't even know existed.

Enjoy the journey, and take your students with you. Build a cathedral or two along the way.

8

Kids We Lost and Kids We Found

Death and Life in the Classroom

We don't win them all. Sometimes, in spite of our best efforts, kids get hurt and we are helpless to protect them. Sometimes, students die, killed by the rampant violence in our society or by a disease that snatches them from us too soon. And sometimes they live. Sometimes they find their spirits just in time. And sometimes we are able to rescue them, to offer them the lifeline they need before it's too late.

Occasionally, a story of a child can only be captured through a poem. I started writing poetry as a means of expressing my frustration over lives I could not change, over situations in the lives of some of my students that were larger than both of us. Nina, for example, was abused by her father. She was twelve. I found out through essays she wrote in class. She was fearful of male teachers and the hormone-laced boys she went to class with. She wrote about guilt, misery, and shame. I reported the abuse, and her father

promptly moved her to another state. I lost her forever. This
is for you, Nina, wherever you are.

Nina

am i bad? am i bad? is he mad? am i glad?
can i breathe? can i dream? can i feel? can i see?

can he come and get me?
will he hate me if i tell?
was i bad to let him touch me?
am i gonna go to hell?

dance with me my agony
brittle on a shelf
dance beyond my misery
lost within myself

tears and pain tears and pain
memories return
dancers never leave the stage
fires always burn

dance away dance away
dance away from fear
spin around spin around
spin and disappear

Carmella was bright and energetic and had a grin that
could melt rocks. In spite of her mother's involvement with
drugs and her father's incarceration, she refused to lose sight
of her dreams. She said her goal was to be a teacher, and
nothing would stop her. But she met Ricardo when she
turned twelve. He was older and charming and so very per-
suasive. She was pregnant the next year. She never finished
high school.

Carmella

At birth, her eyes danced with delight,
Her Mama's smiles,
All in her sight.

At two, her eyes did dance with joy,
A rainy day—a chubby boy,
A bird, a tree—the world her toy.

At four, her eyes danced bright and clear,
At TV shows, at Mama's beer,
At neighbor's curses she could hear.

At six, bright eyes went off to school,
She danced through math, to read was cool,
She loved to think, she learned with ease,
She learned that friends were there to please.

At eight, the dancing eyes are wise,
Seen Mama's pain, and Daddy's dice,
Seen Buddy die, and drug busts twice.

At ten, the eyes dance sad and slow,
So much they have seen, so much they know.
No pirouettes when hot winds blow.

At twelve, the eyes danced through the night,
The music was loud, the stars were bright,
He promised to stay, he left at first light.

At birth, her eyes danced with delight
Her Mama's smiles, all in her sight. . . .

So many of our children get involved in sexual activity
way too early. We see it happening and are helpless to save
them. They are seeking validation and verification for their
existence on the planet. They are seeking peer acceptance.

They are copying their parents' behavior. Whatever the reason, the problem is a whirlwind, swirling out of control. Sometimes the children talk to us, even ask for counsel, although they rarely heed our advice. Trixie was one such child. Petite and pretty, she needed more than someone to tell her that she was loved and appreciated. She had dreams of magic and romance, but all she found was pain and shame.

Trixie—Sex Education

it's not at all like they show it in the movies
where it is a VERY BIG DEAL

no violins play melodies that sweep
with majestic spectacle
no sound track with a subtle rhythm
or filters on the lens
to smooth the edges of the reality

only the rumble of the latest CD
and the squeak of the thin mattress
that smelled of thin regrets

he told me I was special
the only one
a really big deal
the one he'd talk about in the morning
in the locker room to his friends

such a good deal I was
dreams and expectations
available tonight only
for a low discounted price

most of the girls do it all the time
so they say
it's no big deal

you're gonna like it he said
close your eyes and pretend he said
it's no big deal
the teacher showed us diagrams and charts
in a book
that never said what to do when it's over
how to get dressed
without looking at his face
or his eyes
or the rest of him
how to act like it was special

when it really was
a sad small story
not really a very big deal
at all

Frederick was fifteen. You could almost watch him grow from day to day. He was always hungry, even though he ate two lunches at school each day. He inhaled food rather than consumed it. He always carried a bag of potato chips (extra large) and a cola in his backpack. His clothes always seemed to be too small, even though they fit the day before. He was clumsy, like a large Saint Bernard, and just as lovable. He would knock over the desks as he walked in, or trip over the shoelaces of his size fourteen shoes. His work was sloppy, his locker an absolute mess. But he was cheerful and pleasant and seemed to understand that one day he would catch up with his body, which always seemed to be a few steps ahead of him. All he talked about was getting his license and learning to drive. That was his defining goal for the tenth grade. He would have been a wonderful adult—kind and understanding and friendly. But he never had the chance to grow up. He died one sunny morning, a few days after he had received his driver's license, on his way to school. A drunk driver who should have been home sleeping off his drinking from the night before, instead had managed to consume a six-pack of beer before breakfast, and killed Frederick with his shiny black Mustang.

Frederick

His voice is so low,
It's down to his toe;
Face full of pimples and grins.
No longer a kid,
Can't do what he did—
He sweats as adulthood begins.

Got a heart full of gold,
Never has to be told
When a warm, loving hug is a need.
His life's goal is to tame
That new video game
Or eat hamburgers swiftly with greed.

Unclear of his way,
Never sure what to say;
He blurts out his thoughts without plan.
But he's never alone
When he talks on the phone—
The weapon that makes him a man.

He's awkward and thin,
Growing strong from within;
His destiny calls and he goes.
Soon the man in the child
Will no longer run wild
But the boy in the man always knows.

Marianna was a solemn child. She rarely smiled. Her homework was always done perfectly, in handwriting so small it was almost invisible. She had no friends that I was aware of. She did not seek any, nor did any of the other students attempt to reach out to her. Like her handwriting, she was almost invisible. Attempts to reach her failed. She was polite and obedient, but refused to do more than was required in the classroom. She cried easily. Parent conferences, counselor meetings, attempts to bring her out of her shell—all failed. It's easy to overlook a child who desperately wants to be ignored. We all did. She attempted suicide in the seventh grade. Her parents found her in time and she received professional help, but for how long? What despair must hide deeply in her soul? What will happen the next time? I wrote this poem for her.

Marianna's Blues

I heard about the blues, and I think that's what I've got
But I'm not really sure what that means
I know that I like all the colors blue can be
Blue like whimpers, blue like worry, blue like jeans.

If we didn't have the blues, we couldn't see the stars
We couldn't see a rainbow in the sky
No gold or red or purple; no orange, pink or green
Just shadows hugging raindrops as they sigh.

The top of a mountain knows the valley's below
The darkness of night knows the day
The blues that I'm feeling will soon turn to gold
And laughter or light paint my way.

I heard about the blues, and I know that's what I've got
And I don't really care what that means
I know that I like all the colors blue can be
Blue like velvet, blue like ocean, blue like jeans.

Fortunately, not all of the stories end in death and despair. Most of our students survive. Many of their stories are wonderfully funny and refreshing. To hear them tell their tales is always a delight. A big, burly senior named Deshawn told me one day about the time he tried to pick up some cute girls on a Saturday night, and it turned out that that the women in the car were old enough to have been *my* mother! He had the whole class rolling as he told his tale. I wrote this one for him. It's called, "Old Lady Sadie and the Chicken Wings."

It was Saturday night and the time was right
For youngbloods to be on the prowl;
He was driving around, just passing through town
Getting hungry and wearing a scowl.

He looked to his side, and coming up wide
Was a shiny red Caddie DeVille;
Through dark tinted glass came the radio's blast
As it rushed past him, speeding uphill.

He knew they were cute, so he gave hot pursuit
'Cause the license plates read, "FOXY FOOL."
They stopped in a while, and he gave them a smile,
And their door opened slowly and cool.

Dressed in hot pants of red, gray braids in her head,
Was a woman at least sixty-nine.
And with her inside, not trying to hide
Were her partners, all aging, but fine.

"What's happenin', my sweet? Let's go out to eat,"
She said as she checked out his car.
"You willin' to pay? We willin' to play.
There's a chicken place not very far."

He'd been looking for fun, and was really outdone
To be picked up by the gray-headed crew.
But he had money to blow, so he figured he'd go,
And hoped he'd see no one he knew.

So to prove his defeat they drove down the street
To a place called Marie's Chicken Parts.
They got wings and chips, then licking their lips,
They talked of their lives and lost hearts.

The oldest was Sadie, a foxy old lady,
Who was cheerful, outspoken, and large.
It was Sadie's red car, but she never went far
Without Fannie, Viola, and Marge.

Now Fannie was thin, but no one could win
In an arm wrestling contest with her.
Ms. Marge was real cute in her pink jogging suit,
And Viola was wrapped in a fur.

"We're out on a run, and just out for fun,"
They said as they gobbled those wings;
"The world treats you cold when you start to get old,
"But we ain't lost the joy that life brings."

They talked for an hour; of women and power,
Of men, and of learning to fight,
Then they said, "It's been real"; he got thanked for
the meal,
And they left and drove into the night.

Most of our students manage to succeed in one way or another—through laughter, tears, and determination—all of them miracle children. Max, who overcame bone cancer in his leg. They told us his left leg would have to be amputated, but he responded to treatment, miraculously, and except for a slight limp, he will be fine.

Tracy, who was on her way home from school, hurrying to get off the street where gangs had been known to roam, and where gunshots often erupted. Tracy was shot and was not expected to survive. But she did. She graduated with her class and plans to go to college to major in social work so she can help the next generation of kids in her neighborhood.

Leo, the joker who got on my nerves with his foolishness and hyperactivity, now works with the elderly and gives them something to smile about.

Michael, who fell off a ladder while helping his dad paint the house, suffered a concussion but was back at school in a couple of weeks. Christine, whose house burned down, came back to school in borrowed clothes and with a renewed sense of understanding for the misfortunes of others. All of these young people, and hundreds like them, are survivors. They are truly miracles.

Miracle Child

I'm a miracle child
Dressed in black,
I'm dark sweet licorice—
An ebony-melt snack.

I'm a miracle child
Dressed in brown,
I wear cocoa and fudge
And a chocolate gown.

I'm a miracle child
Dressed in tan,
I sizzle bronze steam
In a crunchy-baked pan.

I'm a miracle child
Dressed in gold
I'm honey-bright liquid
Sweet in caramel rolled.

I'm a miracle child
Dressed in cream—
I'm fluffed and I'm sprinkled
Wrapped in sugar-dipped dream.

I'm a miracle child
Baked with smiles on my face,
I'm grilled to perfection
Dipped in gravy and grace.

I'm a miracle child.

9

Finding Your Joy

The Little Things and the Big Picture

oes anyone have any questions?" I asked the class of sixth graders in a middle school. They asked the usual questions—"How old are you?" "How long does it take to write a book?" "What authors do you like to read?" "Can you put me in your next book?" I love the gentle sparring that takes place when they toss questions at me and I toss them back with a witty but honest response.

Then one little girl in the back of the room raised her hand. She was skinny, with hair that looked like the straw in a broom.

"Where do you find your joy?" she asked.

Stunned, I said nothing for a moment. Surely this was a question that her teacher had given her to ask. But the teachers standing near her looked as awed and dumbstruck as I. It was as if they had never seen her before.

She waited quietly, and the other students shifted nervously in their seats.

"What exactly do you mean?" I asked, stalling for time.

"Just what I said," she said quietly. "I want to know, where do you find your joy?"

The question, oddly worded and showing a depth of understanding of life far beyond her eleven or twelve years, made me somewhat uncomfortable.

Finally I looked right at her and said, "That's a powerful question you're asking, and one that can't be answered quickly or easily. I think philosophers have been trying to figure that one out for centuries. But for me, I think I find my joy in the fact that I am blessed enough to live my dreams. I get to write, travel, and talk to students and teachers, and that is what makes me happy. That's what gives me joy."

I thanked her for asking such a thought-provoking question, then challenged her classmates and teachers to think about the answer to her question for themselves. But even after the students had returned to their classes, the question hung in the air like smoke. Where do you find your joy? What is joy?

I often ask that question now when I travel to schools and conferences. The answers are often not what might be expected.

A seventh-grade girl: "I think joy is movement—anything so I'm not stuck in the same place. I want to dance. I want to dance away from here."

A ninth-grade boy: "Joy is being cool. But not showing it off."

A school nurse: "Joy is a day without a sneeze. Joy is free hugs."

A sixth-grade teacher: "A snow day. Kids don't realize we love them as much as they do."

A retired teacher: "Folks who don't complain, but get out there and try to make a difference give me joy. I thank the old soldiers who fought the battles so I could find my joy."

A high school social studies teacher: "Joy exists in our own small worlds. It shows itself when it is shared with others."

A fourth-grade teacher: "Joy is parents who don't give up. Their kids don't give up either. I can find my joy if they just don't give up."

A tenth-grade English teacher: "Words are my joy. I love words and how they decorate a page. And I love showing that to kids."

A high school biology teacher: "Joy is walking in the woods in the fall, enjoying the colors of the leaves, all alone. No students. No interruptions. Just peace and silence."

An elementary school librarian: "Books. The smell of books, the texture of the pages. And the smile on a student's face when they discover that joy."

A college student (education major): "My greatest joy will come when I can finally stand in my own classroom in front of a room full of kids. That will also be the day of my greatest fear."

A middle school principal: "I find joy in the little things that work—bells, clocks, sixth graders."

A junior high school guidance counselor: "Joy is a day without a meeting, or a report, or a problem. Joy is a day where kids come to me with good news. Those days are rare, but they happen. That's why they bring me such joy."

An elementary school reading teacher: "Joy is when they get it. They make the connection. Their little lightbulbs blink on and I helped them plug them in. That's power, and that's joy."

The power and the joy of helping kids make a connection is always there, right around the corner, just down the hall, just at the end of the week, or the month, or the school year. Rarely do we open our hands and find it sitting there, waiting to be acknowledged and enjoyed.

Marvella teaches in a high school in Brooklyn. The building is old and deteriorating and the students come from homes with more problems than can be imagined. But they grin and say, "Yo!" when they see her in the halls or the subway, and they sit up and pay attention when she walks into her classroom. She offers them hope. They give her inspiration.

When I asked her where she finds her joy, she told me, "I know I can't reach all of them. But every one I reach is a victory, because maybe that one would not have made it without me. That's what gives me joy."

Ricardo teaches in a middle school in Los Angeles. Fifteen different languages are spoken by the student body; English is the language least spoken or understood. Ricardo tutors his students before and after school and during his lunch period. They come to him with their problems, their worries, and their dreams. They leave him proud as well as prepared.

When I asked him where he finds his joy, he told me, "Joy is going home in the evening. I sleep well because I do what I love. Other people make more money, but no one gets more satisfaction than I do. I'd rather work with kids than make a million dollars doing a job that has no meaning in my life. I get joy every day. I feel sorry for people who don't."

Frank teaches in a suburban high school in Chicago. His students come from wealthy parents who have given their children the best of everything since childhood. They have money, cars, the latest computer and video equipment, the name-brand clothes. But they share the same adolescent insecurities of young people all over the country, the same fears about the future, about who they are as human beings on this earth. Frank listens and guides. He shares his passion for the world community with them. He takes them to volunteer in the city. He teaches them humility.

When I asked him where he finds his joy, he told me, "Every year my students give a holiday party for the kids in the homeless shelter downtown. They share not just physical gifts but their spirits and their souls with others who are less fortunate. The joy I get is not from seeing the looks on the faces of those that receive the gifts, but the looks on the faces of my students, who have learned to give of themselves. They learn that the world is very small and that we all live in it together. If they have learned to be a better human being because of me, then I have done my job."

Teaching is often maligned and denigrated by the media and the general public for being a thankless job that offers no rewards. If it had no rewards we wouldn't do it. But often we need to be reminded of the small pleasures and simple joys of working with young people, to overshadow the negativity we see portrayed about our profession.

- A kindergarten Show and Tell with ten stuffed animals, three goldfish in a plastic bag, one mother's best china bowl, and one lost lizard.
- A first-grade holiday play with paper costumes and forgotten lines and parents taking pictures and the dragon getting scared and throwing up on the stage.

- A second-grade math class where the concepts can still be learned by counting and manipulating rods and blocks, and where students see success in their hands.

- A third-grade track meet where no one runs very fast or very far, but they run with gusto and delight, mimicking Olympic athletes as they cross the finish line.

- A fourth-grade field trip to a papermaking factory where they drag their coats and gawk with amazement at a process they had never contemplated before.

- A fifth-grade roller-skating party with student skill levels strewn between extremes of timidity and stunts as they roll around the rink, passing each other and catching up, finding their place among their peers and in the larger world.

- A sixth-grade dance where the music is loud and the boys ignore the girls and the girls dance with each other and no one has any fun at all until the very last dance when it is time to go home and they lose their inhibitions and dance like there is no tomorrow.

- A seventh-grade gym class where tall, skinny girls play basketball with short, pimply boys and all of them would rather be home watching television than sweating in a gym class with the opposite sex.

- An eighth-grade band concert where the trumpet and saxophone players, who just picked up those instruments for the first time sixth months ago, manage to play together and produce a tune that is almost recognizable.

- A ninth-grade art class where artistic skill is finally noticed and artistic expression is rewarded and the balance between academics and arts is valued and recognized as necessary for success.

- A tenth-grade home-economics-class meal of carefully snapped fresh green beans, overly cooked roast beef, partially cooked fresh yeast rolls, and a cake with lumpy icing and a partly burned edge—all delicious and proudly shared.

- An eleventh-grade pep rally where the cheerleaders frenetically cheer for the macho males, who take their places as warriors of the field, and where roaring crowds fill the gym with more noise than is necessary, but the joy of being out of class on a warm Friday afternoon before a big game is worth the exuberance regardless of personal feelings about sports or football or competition.

- A twelfth-grade graduation as still-wrinkled, fresh-out-of-the-wrapper caps and gowns rustle in the evening air and "Pomp and Circumstance" is played by the school orchestra and proud smiling faces walk exultantly to the stage, forgetting their kindergarten fears, as well as their adolescent inadequacies, and their high school difficulties. They don't recognize the teachers who walked them down that aisle for the past thirteen years. They see only success and a bright future. And so they should.

Our joy comes in knowing that because of teachers, students walk proudly down that aisle. Because of teachers, students are prepared to face whatever comes.

Sometimes it's hard to see the big picture—how we figure in the vastness of educational goals and curriculum concepts. How can one teacher, working in one small school in one district in one state, ever claim to make a difference in the millions of students that march toward us each September and leave us, sometimes having marched over us, the following June? How do we do know if it matters? I am reminded of a story of a place where no one could see the big picture, until a child showed them.

In a village far, far away—or maybe right over the next hill—were made the most beautiful tapestries in the world. Intricately designed and delicately stitched in a rainbow of colors and patterns, the tapestries told tales of damsels and kings and monsters and heroes. Spun into the silken threads themselves were dozens of stories and verses that told of the past, of the origins of life, and of bright futures yet to be dreamed. Each tapestry was unique and each told a different tale. All of them were beautiful and highly prized. Travelers would come from all over the world to purchase the beautiful weavings in the village square.

The children of the village, whose job it was to sell the tapestries, were also the tellers of the tales, the creators of the stories. People clustered in rapt attention as the children boldly told the tale of the tapestry for sale that day. The tapestries, like the tales, were bits of woven magic, and always sold for a very high price.

When the children reached adolescence, they graduated from the marketplace to the factories where the tapestries were woven. It was a sign of approaching adulthood and a great honor to be tapped to go and actually make the famous weavings.

Anya, one of the best storytellers in the village square, reported with great excitement to the doors of the great tapestry factory on the Monday following her tapping. She could not wait to add her designs and ideas to the great weavings, and to add her stories to the pictures being created with the silken threads. When she entered the factory, she found it strangely silent and subdued. No music played in the background; no sunshine fell through the shuttered windows.

Anya was given a place to sit near a wall. On the wooden table in front of her she found a spool of red silk thread and a pattern. "Follow the pattern," she was told, "and weave only where the red silk threads itself through the tapestry. Then pass it on to the person next to you who will weave the green silk through the tapestry."

Anya was confused. The thread, long and easily tangled, seemed to have no place in the naked rug, which felt heavy and lifeless in her hands. It was not at all like the beautiful finished weavings about which she told her masterful tales. She wove for hours, running strands of red silk thread through rug after rug, never seeing the finished product. Finally she could take no more.

"I don't get it," she declared boldly to the adults in the dark weaving room. "Is this all I get to do—weave the red silk threads in a tapestry that has no meaning to me? When do I get to see what it looks like when all the threads are woven together?"

"We just weave the threads," they told her. "We never get to see the big picture."

"Well, that's dumb!" Anya declared. "I refuse to work in a place that has no sunlight and no music. And I demand to see the tapestry when it is finished! My red silk thread is vital, but no more important than the green and the peach and the lavender threads. All of us together make these weavings, and all of us deserve to see the finished magic our individual threads make."

The adults in the factory, who had always felt that way, but had never had the nerve to voice their opinion, cheered as Anya spoke. One ran to open the windows so the sunlight could stream into the weaving room. Another ran to find musicians to play music for them as they worked. The oldest woman there brought out a newly finished tapestry and carefully unrolled it in front of Anya.

"Tell us the story, Anya. Tell us a tale of mystery and magic. Remind us what the weaving is all about."

And so she did. After that day, the best of the story-tellers was always invited to the pleasant, sunny factory to inspire the weavers and share the tales that bound them all together.

We are weavers of silken threads, makers of magic and dreams. We must look beyond the threads we weave daily, beyond the difficulties of making the threads blend, and into the intricate patterns of the finished tapestry, where our joy is illuminated, and our passions are decorated; where we are a small but vital part of a well-told tale, a story of mystery and magic. We must never forget what the weaving is all about. We must never forget the joy.

10

The Keys to Success

Keys to the Cabinet and Understanding

W e are out of paper for the copier!" the young teacher, Miss Daniels, yelled across the workroom. "Does anyone have any paper in their classroom?" She was greeted with silence. It was the beginning of fourth quarter. Supplies were running low and nothing would be ordered until the new school year in September. If anyone had some paper hidden in a closet, it was a secret stash, a treasure to be guarded with swords and arrows. Exams were coming soon and paper for the copier was almost as precious as toilet paper, which had also run out in the school bathrooms.

"Why don't you ask Old Grizzly?" suggested Mr. Bexley, the good-natured math teacher. "If you dare!"

"You better quit talking about Miss Griswold like that, Bexley!" Miss Winston, the gym teacher, replied sharply. "You ever wonder why you never get your phone messages? Miss Griswold knows who respects her and who doesn't!"

Miss Griswold was the school secretary. She stood six feet tall, had long curly brown hair, and her voice growled with thunder and authority. Only the bravest whispered the dreaded nickname of Old Grizzly—no one had ever dared to say it in front of her. First graders as well as teachers with thirty years experience trembled when she entered a room, although she rarely left her office. Children and staff came to school on time rather than listen to a lecture from Miss Griswold. Parents knew they could depend on her to know exactly where every single child was located in the building at every single minute of the school day.

She ruled her office with an iron fist. She collected all money, kept the accounts perfectly balanced, and made sure flowers were sent to staff members who had illnesses or hospitalizations, weddings or funerals. Miss Griswold knew the location of extra desks for classrooms in the fall, the missing drama costumes, and all holiday decorations. And Miss Griswold kept the keys to everything on a huge brass key ring. Miss Griswold had keys to every single classroom, the outside doors, the security system, the staff bathrooms, and, most important, the wooden cabinet behind her desk.

No one knew exactly what was in that cabinet, but over the years she had been known to extract red pencils, rubber bands, jelly beans, safety pins, and wrapping paper; stuffed animals, glasses, facial tissue, and aspirin; videotapes, extension cords, lunch money, and tuna fish sandwiches. It was also rumored that she had the world's largest stash of paper for the copier, but no one knew for sure. She never let anyone see inside her cabinet and she rarely loaned paper, and only at the end of the school year. She had never given out more than thirty-one pieces of paper at one time. And that came with a lecture.

Miss Daniels was a little intimidated by Miss Griswold's reputation, but desperate. She marched to the office door, knocking first. Miss Griswold motioned for her to enter.

"Good morning, Miss Griswold," the young teacher said politely. "I hope you're having a good day."

"Did they send you in here to get paper from me? I know there's none left in the workroom."

"They didn't send me, but I would like to have some paper if you know where I can find some. Please," she added.

"Why?" asked Miss Griswold.

Miss Daniels had not expected that. She hesitated a moment, then replied, "It's for my children. They're collecting new words and I want them to see how well they've done and how far they can still go!" Her face glowed with excitement.

Without a word Miss Griswold turned her massive body to the ancient wooden cabinet behind her. She removed the heavy brass key ring from her wrist, and with a deft rattling and jiggling of the keys, unlocked the door, which swung open so that the contents of the cabinet could not be seen by anyone who stood on the other side of her desk. She emerged seconds later with a half ream of paper—a school record, they said later—and gave it to Miss Daniels. "Teach them well," she said simply, then turned back to her typing. She made no other acknowledgment of the young teacher's presence, not even of the grateful "thank-yous" she whispered as she left the office.

Miss Daniels hurried back to the teachers' lounge, shyly reported her phenomenal success, and triumphantly ran off her word collections for her classes.

Mr. Bexley, not to be outdone, decided that he, too, needed some paper. "So Old Grizzly's in a giving mood today, I see. I think I'll go score me a few sheets too!" He strolled off to the office and sauntered past Miss Griswold's door. He did not bother to knock.

"What's up, Miss Griswold! You're looking good today!" he began. Miss Griswold ignored him and continued her typing. Undaunted, he continued, "Say, I heard you've got some extra paper for the copier. I could use a few hundred sheets if you could spare them. I'd really appreciate it!" He smiled his most charming smile.

"Why?" she asked him.

He paused. "So I can run off my test. It takes a lot of questions to make sure these little darlings can pass one of my tests—I like to give them a long test so at least they can get *some* of them right!" He chuckled.

"Do you *like* your students, Mr. Bexley? Do you *believe* in them?" she asked him without responding to his comments. Miss Griswold gave up nothing without a thoughtful conversation.

Mr. Bexley was almost sorry he had asked for the paper. "They're OK, but you know, it's sometimes hard even to get to know all of them, let alone like them all."

"Why?" she asked pointedly.

"Well, uh, I try, but I see a hundred fifty kids a day. It's a zoo out there sometimes!" He chuckled again, but softly this time.

Miss Griswold did not smile. She turned, unlocked the cabinet, and emerged with one sheet of paper. "You gotta love 'em before you can teach 'em," she said quietly. "And you don't know how to do either." She dared him with her eyes to challenge her. He decided not to and left the office in defeat. He could hear her keys rattling on her arm as she typed.

The keys to success are not necessarily the keys to knowledge and facts and data, but those that open doors of understanding, love, and the passion for teaching. The keys that will unlock young minds are not made of brass, but are made of smiles and effort and love.

Yes, students need to know the date of the Battle of the Bulge, but more important, they need to know *why* the war in which that battle was fought was a turning point for our civilization, and *why* wars are fought at all or have been fought since the beginning of time. Maybe Miss Griswold's "why?" and "why not?" questions were the most important questions ever asked. Sometimes we forget that the key to knowledge is the answer to a very simple question.

Math facts, such as times tables, are fairly easy to memorize, and are probably a good idea for quick and instant recall when doing computations. But unless a student understands *how* and *why* multiplication works, memorizing the facts is ultimately meaningless.

I once met a remarkable little girl who had made up a rhyme for every single fact in the multiplication table, a feat that required an unbelievably complicated series of mental gymnastics—much more brain power than simple rote memorization. Her mind needed connections, so she created her own. "Nine times seven went up in a tree. When he came down he was sixty-three." She had created her own set of keys.

I'm not sure how well this child scored on standardized proficiency tests, but my guess would be not well. She was a creative thinker and learner. Her mind was filled with thoughtful, clever learning devices that would probably slow down her response time, making her answer fewer questions, and therefore score lower than her classmates who had simply memorized the facts without processing the information. Instead of nurturing what could potentially be a great mind, we discourage her abilities, punish her learning style, and stifle her creativity. Is that the purpose of education? What key have we tossed away that could have opened the doors of knowledge for her?

Tests are, of course, an important tool for determining student knowledge and even teacher preparation, but testing as it currently exists in most states serves more to discourage true learning than to encourage it. Indeed, many state and local officials want only to see wonderfully high test scores, assuming high scores mean massive learning. Unfortunately, that is not necessarily so.

Many states have recently incorporated the "third-grade reading guarantee." This means that by the end of the third grade all students will be reading at a certain level. Although I agree that reading levels should be improved, this so-called guarantee is a gallant but impossible goal. All this really does is guarantee, without a doubt, that hundreds, maybe thousands, of children are doomed to be labeled as failures at the tender age of eight.

Why not implement a program that rewards success instead of punishing failure, a school where a child feels like a winner instead of a loser? I visited a junior high school where the entire student body was divided into what could only be described as a caste system—the practicals and the academics. The students in the academic track got better books, better teachers, and better class schedules. The students in the practical track were treated as second-class citizens, their capabilities limited by a system that nurtured lower expectations. I talked to an eighth-grade boy who told me his name was Kevin. He began his conversation with, "Even though I'm just a practical, I read all your books," and he went on to detail, with great excitement, his joy in reading and discovering. But his conversation told me that he had not been *expected* to be a reader or a learner or an educational success. He had managed in spite of the system to go beyond the limits that had been set for him. What kind of schools are these that teach a child that they are less than academic, that they are "just a practical"? And we wonder why test scores are low and student learning is dismally disappointing.

I have no panacea for the ills of American education, for the problems that beset our schools. But I do know one key that will unlock the ancient wooden cabinet of conventional wisdom and conventional failure is a golden one— made of praise, recognition, reward, and validation.

When my youngest son was in the first grade, he was an active, nervous, bouncy, energetic child—more than a handful for any teacher. His teacher was blessed that year with a class full of children like him, and was overwhelmed with the enormity of handling their behavior, let alone teaching them anything. So she implemented a program in which every bad behavior a child exhibited was punished by a sad-face sticker, which was put on a large chart on the bulletin board. Out of your seat—one sad face. Speaking without raising your hand—two sad faces. If a child accumulated ten sad faces in a week, he or she lost recess privileges. Needless to say, by the end of the week, the teacher had just about the whole class kept in for recess. The kids would act up on purpose just to see how many sad faces they could accumulate. It became a game to see who could amass the most sad-face stickers by the end of the day. My son, I hate to admit, was the undisputed winner of sad faces on the chart. She ran out of room on the chart next to his name. I think the final straw was his refusal to come out from under his desk, which he had decided was his fort and where he wanted to do all his work. The other students threatened to join him. He got forty sad faces for that one. He was exultant. She finally called me in for a conference.

Trying to be diplomatic, playing the role of parent in another teacher's domain, trying not to laugh at the mess she had created, and wanting to improve my son's behavior, I made a suggestion. "Why not switch your system around? Instead of giving the students recognition for their negative behavior, why not reward them for good behavior instead? Why not give them happy-face stickers every time they are polite, or stay in their seats for an hour, or raise their hand to speak?"

She looked at me in amazement. The thought of praise and recognition had never occurred to her—she just knew that bad behavior had to be punished. She also knew that she was quickly losing control of twenty-five six-year-olds. They wanted attention and she gave it to them—but for the wrong reasons.

We decided that extreme negative behavior, such as refusing to come out from under one's desk, would, for the time being, be ignored, since the only purpose of doing such was to accumulate sad-face stickers. Instead, she instituted an award system based on good behavior and good grades. Neatly completed class work, improved spelling scores as well as classroom citizenship were all rewarded. Accumulated happy faces resulted in donuts or popcorn or McDonald's gift certificates at the end of the week. It took a few weeks, but one Friday my son came home glowing, triumphantly clutching his certificate for accumulating the most happy faces in the class! All he needed was a little positive reinforcement.

I have seen that system work in entire schools. I met a fantastic principal of an elementary school in which not only all students but also all the teachers on the staff were complimented and praised for success and hard work and even minor improvements. Students who had been labeled as failures were given a reason to continue to succeed because no one would let them give up and every tiny success was rewarded. Teachers who used to come late and leave early reversed that process because they were rewarded with gift certificates and praise and thanks. And not surprisingly, test scores in her school zoomed—not because students were threatened by failure, but because they were encouraged by success. It cost very little money to implement her program, but she held the key to student and staff improvement—praise, recognition, and reward.

The final key to academic success is one that is often discarded by school officials because of devastating budget restraints and financial cutbacks. That key unlocks the door to the music rooms, the art rooms, and the locker rooms.

When costs must be cut, the first programs to be deleted are the ones that nurture creativity and beauty and artistic development, those that nurture the whole child: Art programs that allow children to see the world spatially, music programs that allow them to respond to the world through the mind, physical education programs that allow them to improve their heart function, and by doing so, the functions of their brains. Studies have shown that listening to classical music improves test scores, that artistic expression adds brain cells, and that physical activity improves learning. Yet we cut the heart out of what makes us human in order to make schools more cost-effective. And we wonder why our students are not achieving as we want them to.

We once read a short story in class about a time in the distant future where all mechanical devices in the world had been destroyed, as had all of the birds and most of the beauty that once existed. People survived on only the most basic level of existence. One man found a music box that played songs from a long-distant past. That bit of musical beauty in a world that had lost it forever sparked violence and desperation in the crumbling civilization of the story because the survivors coveted its magic. The question that the story asked was this: Do we *need* the artistic, the creative, the beautiful, to be human? Can we define ourselves as having humanity without it? My students pondered and argued that question for several days, with most of them concluding that the creative part of humanity is indeed necessary for existence. Even those who disagreed had to admit that the ability to have the discussion, the conversation, the argument was in itself a creative expression, and therefore vitally important.

The keys to academic success are not the keys to rote learning, acquiescence, and lowered expectations. The keys to success for our students are made of passion and excitement and creativity. Maybe Miss Griswold had the answer all along. Maybe the ultimate key is in the answer to the questions "Why?" and "Why not?"

11

Frozen Honey

Special Education, Special Educators, Special Children

Very few people take the time to sing the praises of special education teachers. Every day these teachers open their doors and their hearts to students who will never become doctors or lawyers, students who will never get a job or make a living, and students who cannot even hold a pencil or answer a question. I marvel at their patience, their loving skill, and their dedication. Their idea of progress is a remembered task or a newly mastered skill. "She knows her colors—today we have mastered red and blue," or "Today she was able to move all the balls into the box with no help!" Their idea of a good day is a smile or a wave or a hug. Progress in a special education class is like watching frozen honey melt and drip into your waiting palm—agonizingly slow, yet so sweet when it finally happens.

Those special education teachers who deal with the severely disabled know that the safest way to take a wheelchair down a hill is to walk backward, with the chair facing the crest of the hill rather than the bottom of it. They know that bright minds often lie hidden in barely functional bodies and let their students know they understand. They create clever devices, often made themselves out of materials found at home, that help a child lift a spoon to his mouth, or roll her wheelchair herself.

They show children who are deaf how to hear without sounds. They teach children who are blind to see without their eyes. They teach children who cannot walk how to navigate in a hostile word, and children who cannot talk how to communicate and even sing without words. They know the paths that parents have taken to get their children to that first day of school in a special education program—the disbelief, the tears, the guilt, the blame; the questions with no answers; the problems with no solutions; the pain, the struggle, the determination.

My admiration for special education teachers began when my oldest daughter started school. My first child was born on the coldest, snowiest night of the year. A blizzard pummeled the city, blanketing roads and streets with several inches of furious white snow. Winds blew fiercely, making huge drifts of the quickly accumulating icy snow. It was a night to cuddle together in front of a fire, and gaze out the window at the one or two unfortunate people who struggled to drive their cars down the almost-deserted roads. That was the night I went into labor.

It had been an uneventful pregnancy. I was young and healthy and took meticulous care of myself, eating oranges for vitamin C, and walking for exercise to keep my heart and body strong. I continued to teach until my seventh month, then stayed home to take care of myself and prepare for the great event. The baby was eagerly awaited as my husband and I shopped for baby beds, picked out names, and dreamed the dreams of a young couple on the road to parenthood.

The labor pains started suddenly and forcefully. I had been told, of course, by friends and family members about labor pains, but no one had really been able to translate the extreme levels of pain that wracked my body. But I was unafraid—millions, no, billions of women had done this before me, and certainly I could manage to withstand labor pains like all of the other women in the world. As my husband furiously dug our car out of the garage, I found myself crawling around the middle of the living room, amazed at the intensity and frequency of the pains.

Covered with snow, yet dripping with sweat, my husband hurried into the house and helped me into my coat and out into the storm. He set me gently in the back seat, where I tried not to alarm him as I groaned with each new pain. The streets had not been touched by snow plows during that midnight drive to the hospital. We literally slid by the grace of God down those impassible roads to the doors of the hospital, where I was rushed into the delivery room.

I was asked questions I could not answer, given medications I never asked for, and prepped for delivery. This was long before fathers were welcomed into the delivery room, so my husband paced nervously in the waiting area.

I remember nothing of the delivery. All I know is when I regained consciousness, my husband, standing next to a confused-looking doctor, tearfully told me that the baby, a girl, had serious problems and might not live. Grasping to make sense of what should have been so routine, I could not comprehend why my baby, of all the babies in the world, should not be born healthy and normal.

She was rushed from the hospital where she had been born to a special neonatal care unit at Children's Hospital, so I could not even see her until I was discharged a few days later. All of the other mothers on the floor had their babies brought to them several times a day. I could only turn my head to the wall and cry.

I finally saw her when I was discharged, a tiny, helpless little princess hooked up to wires and machines.

She wasn't a preemie, but she had not breathed as she should and still could not breathe well on her own. She was beautiful. We named her Wendy.

After three weeks in intensive care, Wendy came home to a loving family with high hopes and great expectations that all of her difficulties were in the past. But it was not to be. As she got older and I began to notice the development of other babies, it was apparent that she was not meeting the developmental milestones of childhood. She could not hold her head up or roll over when other babies could. She couldn't sit up or stand. She did not walk.

It took years to get a final diagnosis—they called it cerebral palsy—in order to give a name to a condition that meant that her brain had been damaged at birth, that she would never walk or talk or function like other children. But she had a deep, engaging smile, a quick wit, and a bright, curious mind. It was very hard for her to make her wants or needs known, but she understood so much more than outside observers were aware of. She knew exactly what day and time her favorite TV shows came on, could remember birthdays and special occasions better than I could, and even laughed at dirty jokes right on cue. But she was confined to a wheelchair, and she could only watch other children run and play and develop.

When she started school, we met wonderful, loving teachers and therapists. We learned the vocabulary—"mainstreaming," "inclusion," and "accessibility." She learned that the world no longer revolved around her and that someone other than her mother could care for her. Her world was limited, but a window opened for her that had previously been unavailable. She loved it.

Over the years, I learned to be comfortable with numerous kinds of special schools and programs, as well as with children of all ability levels. One day I was asked to speak at a school for severely disabled students. Schools are often blamed, sometimes with justification, for placing children in special education classes unfairly and for using special education classes as a "dumping ground" for students with behavior problems. But this was not the case here. This was a school designed for kids who were in need of extraordinary amounts of additional assistance, who could not function in a regular classroom.

The teachers made a big deal of me and all my honors and recognition, but I told them that *they* were the true heroes of education. Rarely recognized and often ignored, these teachers are the ones who should get special recognition, who should be honored by politicians and presidents. Special education teachers are the ones who take the children that no one else is willing to take, and they love them and teach them what each child is able to absorb.

The room we were in was full of students, teachers, and aides. There was almost one adult for every student. Some were in wheelchairs, some used walkers, and some were confined to rolling beds that had been wheeled into the room for the occasion. A few wore helmets designed to protect their heads in case of seizures. Others wore bibs or slings or braces. Some made lots of noise, grunts, or squeals of excitement. Others looked past me, seemingly unaware of my existence or the existence of anyone else.

I was unsure how to begin my presentation. I looked at a pretty little girl in a wheelchair—dainty and delicate—who reminded me of Wendy when she was that age. The child smiled at me with her whole face, and it was as if I could see into her soul. She knew who she was, knew her limitations, knew even of the frustrations that she would have to endure. But that didn't matter to her at this moment in time, for today she was here to listen to me.

I told them stories. I sang songs to them. Some sang with me, some clapped, but most of them just sat there, seemingly unmoved by me at all. The teachers took the hands of the students in their own and helped them clap a rhythm to the songs. The teachers wiped runny noses and drippy mouths, they whispered in the ears of those that needed encouragement, they cheered with enthusiasm for those children who could not. It was the teachers who shared that experience with those students and gave it life for them. When the presentation was over, and they were wheeled back to their classrooms, they were smiling and happy. Some of what we had done in that room had slipped from me, through their teachers, and into the hearts of those children. The little girl who looked like Wendy was one of the last to leave. As her teacher wheeled her out of the room, she managed to say "Bye-Bye" to me. A jerky, uncontrolled wave followed. She had not stopped grinning with pleasure for the entire hour that I was there. I waved back as she left the room. Her smile haunted me for a long time.

At another school a couple of years later, I was asked to speak to all of the students in the seventh grade at a general assembly. Later, the teacher informed me, they had chosen several students from the "enriched" classes to have special writing workshops with me. That's all I needed to hear to get me going.

"Enriched kids?" I asked. "What does that mean?"

"Oh, you know, the ones who love to read and write, the kids from the advanced classes. The ones who would most benefit from a one-on-one with you."

"Do you have any kids who hate to read and write?" I asked.

She laughed nervously. "Of course."

"Do you have any bad kids, any discipline problems?"

"A few, I suppose, but they won't bother you. We have made sure they are not in the assembly and they certainly won't be in the small group discussions." I suppose she assumed I was worried that some of those harmful kids would find their way into my presence.

"Do you have any special education classes here?"

"Oh yes, of course. But they won't bother you either. The students in those classes sometimes make strange noises and are distracting in an assembly, so we have arranged to keep them away as well."

"Most seventh graders make strange noises at one time or another," I told her wryly. "I want the kids from that special education class in the very front row, and the kids that you consider to be discipline problems right behind them. And in that small group session, I don't want to talk to the 'enriched' kids that love to read and write. I want to talk to those kids who hate reading and writing. Perhaps I can inspire them to get interested in books, or show them how they can express themselves though writing. Those are the kids that need me more."

She was amazed and I suspect more than a little irritated with me, but she agreed, and we had one of the best assembly and workshop sessions I have ever conducted.

When I got to the school that day, a tall boy with braided hair and baggy pants waited at the door with two of his friends. They were almost dancing with excitement. As soon as I set foot inside the door, he approached me.

"You Miss Draper?"

"Yes, I am," I told him.

"It's her! It's her! She's here!" he shouted to his friends. "Let's go tell Miss Johnson." They took off down the hall, running at full speed and leaving me standing there alone at the door.

I smiled and proceeded to the main office where I announced myself. By this time the threesome had returned triumphantly with Miss Johnson.

"See! I told you she was here. I found her first. She shook my hand!" declared the tall young man, whose name was Jo Jo.

Miss Johnson told me later that Jo Jo was in the special education class, had major learning disabilities and, probably as a result, also tended to be a discipline problem. But she had never seen Jo Jo so excited. He had never been invited to an assembly and had never been allowed to get up close and personal to anyone like a writer before.

The students that had been predicted to be discipline problems were perfectly behaved, Jo Jo included, listening raptly to my silly stories on stage. At the workshops, we opened doors that had been previously closed and let a little light in some windows that had been nailed shut. The special education students were so appreciative I had invited them to the assembly that, with the encouragement of their teachers I'm sure, they wrote me letters later, laboriously written, to thank me for including them in the program.

Jo Jo was my enthusiastic guide throughout that day. Before I left I gave him a signed copy of one of my books for his own. He grinned and promised to read it right away. I have no doubt that, in spite of his learning difficulties, that is exactly what he did.

The United States has many critics of its education policies and practices, but unlike other countries, who often ignore the disabled, we attempt to educate all children, even those that are seemingly uneducable. Of course there are weaknesses and faults in the system, but children who would never reach their full potential, whatever that might be, are at least given the opportunity to be the best that they can be.

Because of the terrible increase in drug and alcohol use, babies are born addicted, born with fetal alcohol syndrome, born with mental or physical challenges. Through no fault of their own, they are thrust into a world that demands and celebrates perfection, a world where the best and the brightest are made our heroes, a world where the least and the weakest are left in the silence of the shadows. It is in that world of shadows where special education teachers live. Whether they teach children with minimal dysfunction or maximum disability, these teachers should be honored, lauded, and recognized.

The greatest need for the next generations are teachers who are willing and able to teach special education, teachers who are willing to work for small joys and tiny rewards, teachers who can gain satisfaction from a job well done and do it every single day with little proof of success, teachers who teach with both skill and love. They are a rare and precious commodity and I will always be thankful for their presence on this earth.

My daughter Wendy will never be a scholar or a seamstress. She will never drive a car or walk down the aisle in marriage. She will never tell me that she loves me, at least not in words. But she gives the best hugs and has the biggest smile in the world. She is a happy, well-adjusted, intelligent young woman who loves music and books and stories. For Wendy and for all of the other children who cannot, I offer my sincere thanks and praise to the special educators who cared for her and who care for them.

12

The Last Day of School

Remembering the Dreams
and the Dreamers

The last day of school is always difficult. Lockers have been cleared, and the halls echo strangely, as if the stuffing, the insulation has been removed from the plastered walls. In a way I guess it has. All of the books and papers and winter coats and notebooks and dreams and possibilities have been removed, leaving only scratched paint and cookie crumbs.

The classroom is bare. All the posters have been taken down and carefully rolled to be used again. The colorful bulletin boards are now merely bare slabs of spongy material, dull and littered with lost staples and thousands of punctures from years gone by. The samples of student work, once so proudly displayed, have been tossed unceremoniously into book bags or folders, some never to be seen again—memories of past successes as well as failures, memories of accomplishments and learning.

The remnants of yesterday's party have been swept into the wastebaskets, which overflow with the papers and thoughts of the past year. The class rabbit has found a new home and the plants have been stuffed in the trunk of my car since yesterday.

The room feels hollow. Echoes and shouts bounce like stray bullets, with no softness of color on the walls to blend them smoothly into the fabric of the day. Desks, where children now sit out of habit rather than necessity, scrape loudly on the scuffed floors, as if coughing with despair at the thought of the upcoming separation.

There is very little to say as we wait for the last bell to ring. Exams are over, grades have been turned in to the office, and their immediate futures, either in summer school or at the swimming pool, have already been determined. Some of the children boast loudly of summer plans, while others, overcome with the finality of the day, sit quietly, perhaps staring out of the window, waiting for the start of the next phase of their lives. There is a familiarity between them as classmates, a comfort level they feel with each other and with their teacher, the one they both loved and hated.

As I observe them, I marvel once again at how much they have changed since the first day of school. Ben has grown five full inches taller. Margarita, flat-chested in September, is suddenly dangerously voluptuous. Kenny's mom died. Lynn had surgery after an automobile accident. Holly moved away in October and transferred back in January. Lucy and Randall discovered each other. Carlos got glasses. Jeff got pimples. Terry still can't spell. Lauren is the most prolific reader. Roger is dyslexic and reads very poorly. Denise and Trina and Liz failed the state proficiency test; all of them felt defeated by its enormity. Max and Fred learned to like poetry. Christine discovered she is a wonderful writer; she scribbles in a notebook constantly now. Susan's artwork won a national award. Clifford won a swimming contest. Arthur's family, who live by the river, lost everything in the spring floods. The entire class learned about social responsibility as they all helped to get his family back on their feet.

Tawana discovered her talent and love for the trumpet; she had wanted to play the flute, but all of them had been taken when instruments were distributed, so she ended up with the trumpet by default and she loved it. Marco quit biting his fingernails. Justine got in trouble for stealing books from the public library. Derek has decided he wants to go to college to study music instead of joining a rock band; his mother is very thankful. Bonnie tasted Shakespeare for the first time and discovered a thirst for more. Lou, who is in a wheelchair, dreams only of being a doctor. Leo discovered he loved being on stage; he talks of Hollywood and big dreams.

Dreams are so much easier than reality. We dream of winning the lottery, of losing weight, of winning on *Jeopardy*, of teaching every single child everything he needs to know. Children are natural dreamers. They still believe in the magic.

I remember a student named Vincent—the ultimate dreamer. He lived down the street from a friend of mine. What was Vincent like when he was seven? When his teacher passed out crayons, Vincent colored with red and green at the same time, and he colored outside of the lines—always. When the teacher asked for the capital of Ohio, Vincent said "O." When the teacher asked what was eleven plus one, Vincent said, "one hundred eleven." He was never ever right, but he was never completely wrong. Vincent was labeled as difficult, disobedient, dyslexic, and dumb. Nobody ever labeled him as a dreamer.

Vincent drifted through school, unconcerned about the rules and restrictions. He was suspended for lighting a match near the sprinkler system. He was pleased that he had proved the school safe for his friends; it did not occur to him that what he was doing was wrong. He justified his actions for himself and that, to Vincent, was sufficient. Another time he slept all night with some homeless people he had befriended downtown. The fact that he had not bothered to call his mother and tell her what he was doing did not occur to him until he saw his picture on the morning news as a missing child. He told his mother later, "I wasn't missing. I knew exactly where I was."

When a tornado hit our town, and dozens of homes were destroyed, Vincent was one of the first to volunteer to help. He organized groups of his friends to collect and sort donated goods for the families. Many people had no lights, no power, no homes, and no hope. They could see no way out of their terrible situation. They needed the magic of a dream. Vincent jumped right in and showed the people how to make positive soup from negative ingredients, how to find hope in togetherness. Vincent the dreamer was finally recognized and appreciated. I think he received a citation from the mayor.

Another dreamer I met was a little boy who lived in Alabama. I had the opportunity to talk to a group of seven-year-olds about their school. He was chubby and had a frown on his face the whole time I spoke to the group, as if he were really puzzled about something. He didn't ask questions like the other children. He just sat there with his arms crossed in front of his chest, a question mark on his face.

"So, do you like your school?" I asked him.

"I like it fine," he answered in a syrupy Southern drawl.

"And do you like your teacher?"

"Oh, I like her *real* fine!" he said, smiling a little. "She's pretty."

I smiled back. "And you're learning everything she teaches you?" I asked.

"Oh, yes Ma'am," he said, glad that I had brought up the subject, "But there's something that's puzzling me and maybe you can tell me, since you're not from around here," he whispered conspiratorially.

"Sure," I answered carefully, not sure what he was going to say.

"I think there's a whole lot my teacher just ain't telling me! I think she's holding out some important information that I'm gonna need. I got big dreams, you know!"

I stifled my laughter and assured him that he'd get to know everything real soon. That little boy was a dreamer, a thinker, a seeker of knowledge. And he found the courage to ask for answers to his questions. That is what a dreamer does.

The true leaders of a society are the dreamers—the inventors, the scientists, the business tycoons, and the teachers. Yes, the teachers. Who do you think educated the inventors, the scientists, and the business tycoons? Yes, a teacher. It takes big dreams and a whole lot of guts to put ourselves out there in the face of defeat and discouragement—day after day, year after year.

But what about the kids we miss? The kids that fail? The kids whose dreams interrupt their lives? Several years ago, I had a student named Roscoe. He was one of those kids—a dreamer and, seemingly, a problem child.

Roscoe was late for the first day of school. The last bell rang and the halls were empty. Voices of the teachers echoed into the clean, shiny hallways. They talked of supplies, and seating charts and new books—all the information we give on the first day of school. The kids sat quietly, even though they had heard it all before. Roscoe had heard it too, so he decided not to show up for all that first-day stuff. He whistled in the empty hallway and walked into the classroom one hour late.

"Hey, teach'!" he said, smiling. "I'm Roscoe! What's up?" The kids laughed; I frowned.

"Take your seat in the third row, Roscoe," I said. "Why are you so late?"

"Oh, the cartoons were on and I had to get to level fourteen on my video game, so when I finished, I hurried on over here," Roscoe explained with a shrug of his shoulders. He looked unconcerned and picked his nose as he strolled slowly to his seat.

"Roscoe!" I called out sternly. "You will NOT be a disruption to my class! You will sit silently, fill out these forms, and see me as soon as the bell rings!" Roscoe grinned as he took the papers, and seemed very unconcerned with my anger. The rest of kids in the class were quiet, and didn't dare laugh out loud, but they kept looking over at Roscoe's desk as he drew funny pictures on his notebook paper. I frowned and sighed. It was going to be a long school year.

Roscoe continued to be a problem throughout that year. He missed most of his homework assignments, he lost his books, he never studied for tests. But he always had a smile on his face, and he always seemed to be having so much fun. When I took the class to the library, the other kids searched for a book for their book report. Roscoe read a car magazine and made zooming noises like a racing car. Sometimes I asked students to go to the board to do grammar exercises. When it was Roscoe's turn, he drew funny pictures next to his sentence, which was always wrong. Roscoe could always bring laughter to the class.

I tried many times to contact his parents, but they never returned my calls. Once I got a postcard from his mother. It had a picture of the Statue of Liberty on the front and a New York postmark. Roscoe saw the postcard on my desk and remarked, "She sent me the same card last week."

I asked, "Do your parents travel much?"

"Yeah, my mom's a singer and my dad's a stockbroker. One leaves and the other comes home. When they're both home, they throw cool parties."

"When do they spend time with you, Roscoe?" I asked.

"Whenever!" Roscoe said carelessly. He was practicing throwing paper wads in the wastebasket.

The school year continued, as all school years do. There were tests and homework, assignments and projects, assemblies and field trips, and lots of chances to get lessons done and get a little new information into their heads. Roscoe's parents never did come in for a conference, but Roscoe had more fun than any other student that year. He told the best jokes, made the funniest faces, and could think of the best questions to stall me when I was about to give an assignment.

The end of the school year finally arrived. On Monday of the last week of school, I returned all the end of the year projects to the class. They were proud of the work that had done that school year. Just as the last bell rang, I called Roscoe's name. The rest of the class poured into the hallways, cheering that most of the work for this year was completed. "Roscoe," I said quietly, "your portfolio is empty, your poetry notebook is full of cartoons, and your book report is on a comic book."

"Yeah, I know," Roscoe replied. For the first time he wasn't smiling. "But it's not my fault."

"Yes, it is," I told him gently. "You are the only one who has control of what you will do with your life. I can encourage you or threaten you, but only you can live your dreams."

Roscoe ended up repeating that school year. He fooled around for the rest of his high school years, barely passing, but having lots of fun. You might think that he ended up as a failure in life. But a few years ago, while I was up late grading papers, I was watching the Tonight Show. Who was the special guest comedian? You guessed it—Roscoe! His dreams were not the dreams of everyone else. He had the strength to hang on to them and let them carry him to his own destination. Maybe he listened to me after all.

So, as we wait for the bell to ring and release them into their future and my past, I hope that I have created some dreamers—visionaries who know that to reach the stars it is necessary to build a sturdy ladder of reality. I gave them my best—all that I had. My dream is that they have learned to do the same.

When school starts in the fall, I'll see all of them again, but it will never be exactly the same. The same configuration of wills and spirits and personalities that make up this class at this moment in time will never be repeated. They are unique, like participles dangling in the universe, a permanent adjunct to the composition that is the life of a teacher. Although all of us are aware of this fact, no one verbalizes it.

Next year, another group will replace them. Strangers with their own nuances and idiosyncrasies and dreams. Unknown entities, just as these young people had once been, soon to become friends, just as these young people are today. Still, somehow, I know that no new group of children will ever take the place of these young people who are leaving me today. It is that feeling that helps us to come back every year and try one more time. One more dream. One more possibility. One more dreamer. What a wonderful way to make a living!

Appendix

One Small Torch
Chapter One of *Forged by Fire*

Used by Permission.

"If you don't sit your stinkin', useless butt back down in that shopping cart, I swear I'll bust your greasy face in!" she screamed at the three-year-old in front of her. He studied her face, decided she was serious, and put his leg back inside the cart. He was standing near the front end of the cart, amidst an assorted pile of cigarette boxes, egg cartons, and pop bottles. He didn't want to sit down anyway because of the soft, uncomfortable load in his pants that had been there all afternoon and it felt cold and squishy when he moved too much. He rarely had accidents like that, but when he did, Mama sometimes made him keep it in his pants all day to "teach him a lesson."

Gerald was only three, but he had already learned many such lessons. He'd never seen Sesame Street, never heard of Riverfront Stadium—he didn't even know he lived in Cincinnati. But he knew the important things—like never mess with Mama when she was in bed—Mama got really mad when you woke her up, especially if she had somebody in bed with her. And never touch the hot thing that Mama used to light her cigarettes, even if the mysterious orange and blue fire that comes out of it liked

to tease you and dance for only a moment before running away.

Mama had once caught Gerald playing with the lighter,
and she made the fire come out and she held his hand right
over the flame, but it wasn't his friendly fire dancer, but a
cruel red soldier that made his hand scream and made him
dizzy with pain and he could smell something like the meat
Mama cooked, but it was his hand. When she stopped, she
had washed his hand with cool water and soothed him with
warm hugs and wrapped with salve and bandages the place
where the fire soldier had stabbed him. She told him that she
had done it "for his own good" and to "teach him a lesson."
He had tried to tell her that he was just trying to find the fire
dancer, but she wasn't listening and he had given up, thankful for the hugs and the silence.

One other lesson that Gerald had learned was *never,
never* stay near Mama when she sniffed the white stuff. She
got it from a man named Leroy who smelled too sweet and
smiled too much. When he leaves, you hide behind the
couch and hope Aunt Queen comes over because sometimes Mama yells and gets her belt or her shoe and hits, and
hits, and hits. . . . And sometimes she just goes to sleep on
the floor and it gets dark and you cry and your tummy feels
tight and hurty, but at least there's no shoe to run away
from.

Once Aunt Queen had found Gerald curled up behind
the couch sucking his thumb. His pajamas were soaked and
smelly and he had been shivering and hungry. Mama had
been gone all day. She had told him not to leave the room,
and he had really, really tried to be good, but he was so
cold, so very cold. Aunt Queen had taken him to her apartment and given him a warm bath, a bowl of hot soup, and
some warm, fuzzy sleepers, even though she had to pin the
back of them so they wouldn't fall off. Then Mama had
come and she and Aunt Queen had yelled and screamed so

much that Gerald had to hold his ears while he lay curled on the foot of the bed. Finally Mama started crying and Aunt Queen was saying stuff like, "I know honey," and Gerald knew he was going back home.

That night, Mama had hugged him and kissed him and held him close until he fell asleep. Gerald had felt so warm and special and golden—he wanted to feel like that forever. He knew his Mama loved him. She had bought him a GI Joe man last week and it wasn't even his birthday or Christmas or anything, and most days she combed his hair and dressed him in clean clothes, and told him to say, "Yes, Ma'am" to grown folks. And sometimes, on really good days, she would hug him and say, "You know you're my best baby boy, don't you, Gerald? You know you're my baby, don't you?" And he would smile and that warm, golden feeling would start at his toes and fill him all the way up to his smile.

Even though Mama had yelled at him, today was a good day. Mama always yelled—it was no big deal. (Some days he yelled back at her. Then she would slap him and he'd cry and he'd cuss at her and then she would slap him until his head hurt. So mostly he ignored her.) But today was good day, a shiny day, he thought. The sun was bright gold outside against a clear blue sky. And inside the grocery store there were so many colors and sounds and lights that Gerald just grinned. It was always crowded when they went. Other children would be in carts also and they would have to pass very close to each other. Gerald liked to pretend he was driving a big, fine silver car down the expressway.

Sometimes the cart would be a tank, as he passed cautiously through rows of armed cling peaches and silent sentinels that looked like boxes of frosted flakes. And at the checkout lane, the armies rolled smoothly down the long black road that disappeared under the counter. He started to ask Mama where it went, but it was more fun to imagine that it went to a secret hideout where only sweet potatoes and boxes of oatmeal were allowed.

When they got home from the grocery store, Gerald sat on floor and watched Mama stack the boxes and cans on the shelf. She was whistling—he had never heard her whistle before and he loved the way she laughed as he tried to imitate her. She changed his clothes (and didn't even yell at him for not being a big boy) and gave him two cookies and an apple. Then she went into the other room. When she came out, she had changed her clothes and Gerald thought he had never seen anything so lovely. She had on her sparkly fancy dress that Gerald liked to touch.

"Mama will be right back, baby," she told him. "I just have to go see Mr. Leroy for a minute. You stay right here and wait for me, you hear?" Gerald started to cry, but he didn't want Mama to lose her good mood, so he just nodded and bit his lip. The door closed and he could hear her high heels clicking on the steps. Then it was very, very quiet.

After he finished both his cookies and the apple had turned brown on the white parts, Gerald looked for something to do. It was getting dark and he wanted GI Joe to sit with him because the shadows on the wall were getting long and scary. He found GI Joe on the floor next to Mama's bed, right next to her cigarette lighter that she had been looking for this morning. Gerald picked it up and for a time he used it as a gun for Joe, then it was a log for Joe to jump over, then it was an enemy for Joe to attack.

Finally Gerald started idly flicking the little red handle. At first it just made a scratchy sound and the smell made him cough and remember how he got that had brown place in the palm of his hand. Then he remembered the tiny fire dancer, and he wondered if it still lived in there with the fire-sword soldier.

After numerous flicks, he got the fire to stay on. He grinned with delight. The dancer was there, smiling at him and bowing for him, changing from splendid orange to icy green to iridescent purple. The lighter flame flickered magically, making golden the purple shadows on the wall.

With sudden inspiration, Gerald shouted, "Hey Joe, we got a torch!" as he and GI Joe marched around the kitchen table. Gerald crawled under the table then, flicking the lighter over and over again to light the way for GI Joe. They fought shadows and monsters; they blew up cities and kingdoms. Gerald made the sound effects and GI Joe dutifully followed his general into combat. As the mighty battle came to its climax, Gerald crawled up on a chair and stood on the kitchen table, waving his arms triumphantly. "Mama would kill me," he thought momentarily, "if she saw me up here," but the thought passed as GI Joe fought the terrible mountain man by the light of only a single torch.

Suddenly the tiny light of GI Joe's torch was huge and bright as the tip of one curtain in the window touched the flame. Gerald heard a loud "whoosh" and then he turned in terror to see the whole window covered with harsh red flames that crawled and licked and jumped along the windowsill. Gerald scrambled down from the table and ran to his hiding place behind the couch. "Mama said stay here and wait for her," he told himself. "I know she'll be here in a minute." He peeked around the corner of the sofa and watched flames consume the boxes of cereal and macaroni that Mama had just bought. When the fire reached the bottle of Big K soda, Gerald watched, fascinated, as the soda bubbled, then fizzed. When it finally burst in a loud, sizzling explosion, Gerald jumped back behind the sofa, coughing and wheezing from the heat and smoke.

He curled up in his usual position then, thumb in his mouth, crying softly. He thought about his Mama and how pretty she was. And he wondered if GI Joe would ever find his way back. And he wondered how he could see so many colors with his eyes closed.